Aristotle in Outline

Aristotle in Outline

Timothy A. Robinson

Hackett Publishing Company, Inc.
Indianapolis/Cambridge

Printed in the United States of America

12 11 10 09 08 07   3 4 5 6 7 8

For further information, please address

Hackett Publishing Company, Inc.
P.O. Box 44937
Indianapolis, Indiana 46244-0937

www.hackettpublishing.com

Design by Dan Kirklin

Library of Congress Cataloging-in-Publication Data

Robinson, Timothy A., 1947–
        Aristotle in outline / Timothy A. Robinson.
            p.   cm.
        Includes bibliographical references and index.
        ISBN 0-87220-314-X.   ISBN 0-87220-315-8 (cloth)
        1. Aristotle.   I. Title.
        B485.R49 1995
        185—dc20   94–46137
                                                              CIP

ISBN-13: 978-0-87220-315-0 (cloth)
ISBN-13: 978-0-87220-314-3 (pbk.)

The paper used in this publication meets the minimum requirements of
American National Standard for Information Sciences—Permanence of Paper
for Printed Library Materials, ANSI Z39.48–1984
                                        ∞

Contents

To My Mother
who waited a long time

Aristotle in Outline

Introduction

In 1978, Mortimer Adler published a book entitled *Aristotle for Everybody*. Whatever its other merits or demerits, I think the title is misleading. In my opinion, Aristotle is *not* for everybody. To help you decide whether Aristotle is for you, let me go over the things that a study of Aristotle is good for. If you're reading this not by choice but because it was assigned, these same considerations may help reconcile you to what I know is going to be a strenuous task.

Aristotle is a very systematic philosopher. "Systematic" can mean different things. In Aristotle's case, it means that ideas developed in one area of investigation often find applications in other areas. As a result, his treatment of one topic may not be fully clear until you have examined his discussions of other topics which form a basis for that one. While a work on ethics, for example, can be read with profit by itself, it only becomes fully understandable when you are aware of its presuppositions, some of which are to be found in Aristotle's psychology. And to fully appreciate his reasoning in psychology—reasoning about human nature and about the nature of other organisms—you need to be familiar with his ideas about nature in general, as expounded in his physics. By studying Aristotle, you can learn one of the ways in which a philosophic system can be fitted together. This is worth knowing even if you are not a philosopher but a "general reader." It is worth knowing because of a fact of which many general readers are unaware, namely, that some of our most important beliefs are accepted (or rejected) not by directly testing them against the facts, but by considering the roles they play in systems of belief, only some parts of which can be tested directly against the facts. One reason for accepting a particular system of beliefs is that it pans out at the points where it can be directly tested. But there are other considerations as well, such as whether the system is consistent, whether it is simpler than alternative systems, and whether it can integrate a wider range of data than rival systems. None of these criteria is absolute, and we may tolerate a failure of corroboration at certain points or even an apparent conflict between the system and some of the facts, provided the system scores high enough on other criteria. The general idea is sometimes expressed nowadays by saying that we do not test individual assertions against the facts of experience, but rather it is the system as a whole which is tested, both against the body of facts as a whole, and against the criteria other than correspondence with facts. But this way of putting it is misleading because we do test some individual assertions against experience—how else could we connect the system to experience at all? The legitimate point that this misleading formulation is trying to make is that we evaluate a system in terms of its overall success; a system seldom stands or falls on the result of a single experiment or because of its success or failure in measuring up to a single well-established fact. Furthermore, we generally evaluate a system in comparison to the available alternatives. We will tolerate shortcomings in a system as long as it has fewer or less important shortcomings than its rivals.

To appreciate this contemporary understanding of philosophical systems, and thus to be more sophisticated in dealing with questions of argument, evidence, and the confirmation or refutation of theories, it is necessary to have a sense of how a system of thought fits together. For this purpose, any sufficiently complex system of thought will serve. There is an obvious advantage in selecting for study a system which currently bears the seal of approval of the scientific community, for this system can be taught simply as "The Truth" (since it represents what is currently our best perception of the truth). But in the late twentieth century, that is not so easy to do. In the first place, our most fundamental systems are not widely accessible. Only the mathematically gifted can really comprehend what is going on in quantum theory. Moreover, our systems tend to be fairly narrow in scope. No one has worked out, in a generally acceptable way, the ramifications of quantum theory for psychology or sociology, much less for ethics. Now it must be admitted that much of Aristotle's physics and chemistry is obsolete. No one since Newton (not to mention Einstein) can take them seriously. Nevertheless, even if they are wrong, they are accessible to anyone of normal intelligence. And their applications in other fields have been worked out. A study of Aristotle thus offers advantages for the understanding of systematic thought which the study of contemporary science cannot rival.

To this we should add a further consideration. Popularizers of modern science like to point out that Newton's physics remains valid within a restricted domain; it can be seen to represent a special case under the wider principles of quantum physics, a special physics that remains valid given certain initial assumptions. A similar case can be made, I submit, for Aristotle's science. While his physics may seem feeble or even muddle-headed compared to the masterful manipulations of quantitative data carried out by modern scientists, many of Aristotle's basic concepts—nature, potentiality, and others—remain invaluable for everyday thinking, much of which is nonquantitative. They provide useful tools for coping with the macro-level world we live in. And in most cases, they are merely refinements of the concepts we are already implicitly using. Within certain limitations, Aristotle's science can be said to reflect the ways we think, and perhaps even ways we cannot help thinking.

In sum, our first reason for studying Aristotle is that he represents a case study in systematic thought, and one which is more accessible than many of the alternatives.

A second reason is that Aristotle is a very methodical philosopher. In carving out areas for investigation, in formulating questions, in arriving at answers and in defending them, the procedures he follows are deliberate and consistent, and he has made an effort to describe them for us. And again, these methods are exhibited in the construction of a system which covers a wide range of subject matters and yet remains accessible to the general reader. Hence, anyone who wants to study methodical thinking in one of its best representatives could hardly do better than to spend some time on Aristotle.

A third reason for interest in Aristotle is that his system and his methods, as well as the particular conclusions he reached, have been tremendously influential. From the time of his writing in the fourth century B.C.E., through the eighteenth century C.E., there is hardly a single philosopher in the Western world who does not show some traces of Aristotle's influence. And in some times and places, he set the pattern for how philosophy and science were to be carried out—for example, among Islamic and Jewish philosophers between 800 and 1200 C.E., and among Christian philosophers from 1100 to 1400. (These medieval followers of Aristotle often referred to him simply as "The Philosopher.") During the late Roman period and again during the Renaissance there were prominent schools of Aristotelians. Even during the 1950s in this country, some aspects of his thought were revived by a group of scholars at the University of Chicago who became known as the "Chicago Aristotelians." Aristotle's influence becomes even more significant when you realize that until the twentieth century, there were no clear dividing lines between philosophy and science, or indeed, between philosophy and other academic disciplines, period. Any systematic or critical investigation qualified as philosophy, including the study of literature, history, and economics. Consequently, if you're interested in the culture of any of the periods just mentioned, or if you just want to understand the broad sweep of Western intellectual history, you must have some understanding of Aristotelianism.

Fourth, while many of Aristotle's ideas in physics, chemistry, and biology must be classed as outmoded, his theories of ethics and political science remain viable competitors against more recent theories. These theories have undergone something of a revival in recent years, as ethical theorists have increasingly turned away from their traditional emphasis on rules of conduct and decision procedures in favor of an ethics that emphasizes character, motivation, and the social context of action. (A leader in this revival has been Alasdair MacIntyre.)

In a similar vein, Aristotle's conceptions of the nature of scientific explanation and of the methods for establishing scientific principles are interesting not only as a case study in methodical thinking but also because the former represents an ideal of continuing appeal to many thinkers, and because the latter appears to some to hold promise of resolving problems of knowledge which are insoluble on more recent theories. These dimensions of Aristotle's thought, too, have received their most sustained attention recently from Alasdair MacIntyre.

The fourth reason for studying Aristotle, in sum, is that in the process you'll come across some ideas that are still pretty hot.

My fifth and final reason for looking at Aristotle is a little more nebulous. In a way, it incorporates and enlarges on the first four. In reading Aristotle, you'll encounter a mind of the first rank, and a man with an unrivalled confidence that the patient and painstaking use of our rational powers will eventually lay bare all that there is to know about the world. If there were a church of Reason, Aristotle would be one of the greatest of its saints. Even if you never convert to Aristotle's creed, contact with such a thinker is almost certain to change your perceptions about what reason can do and how it can do it. The German philosopher Novalis described philosophy as the attempt to "domesticate" the world, to come to see it as one's home. One comes away from Aristotle's philosophy with a powerful sense that here, if anywhere, was a person who felt at home in this universe.

Perhaps that is enough to convince you that Aristotle is worth studying. Next, I must help you decide whether this book represents a good way for you to study him. This book is intended primarily for college undergraduates with no previous course-work in philosophy. But I hope it will also prove valuable to graduate students and professional academics who want a quick refresher course on, or a brief introduction to, Aristotle's thought. Among undergraduate students, I have two audiences in mind: those who are reading Aristotle's own works and could use some assistance understanding particular doctrines and seeing how it all fits together, and those who are studying other thinkers or schools influenced by Aristotle and therefore need an overview of the Aristotelian background.

Both audiences include people interested in only one aspect of Aristotle's thought. For their sake, it was desirable to have each part of the book capable of standing on its own. But that would interfere with my aim of exhibiting the systematic character of this philosophy. One could remedy that shortcoming by supplying numerous cross-references and by repeating oneself a lot. But that makes reading tedious for those who do read the whole book. By way of compromise, I have emphasized interconnectedness in the first chapter, dealing with Aristotle's conceptions of wisdom and science, and I tried to write the chapters on ethics and politics so that they could be read independently both of the earlier chapters and of each other.

Many features of Aristotle's philosophy are best grasped by working through several different examples. I have assumed that this book will be used most frequently as a supplementary text in college courses, in which the instructors can provide additional illustrations of points that prove particularly difficult to their students. That sort of thing often becomes tedious when it is done in writing, and it would work against my desire to keep this work concise. I have therefore kept the examples in the text to the minimum necessary for clear exposition. If you are reading this work on your own, I would advise you to play instructor to yourself: imagine different situations on which you can attempt an Aristotelian analysis. For example, survey a variety of changes and try to identify Aristotle's four causes in each of them.

To my mind, the major shortcoming of most introductory surveys of Aristotle (and other thinkers as well) is that they concentrate on the doctrines espoused by the philosopher and neglect the reasons why those doctrines seemed true. And yet almost all philosophers will agree that the reasons why philosophers hold doctrines are more important than what the doctrines are. A major concern for me has been to make it clear to the reader why Aristotle believed what he did. Sometimes this is a matter of summarizing his argument for a particular claim. At other times what is required is to lay out the background assumptions in the light of which a particular doctrine seems plausible.

The ethical and the political thought of Aristotle present particular difficulties in this regard. Aristotle's works on these topics are at first glance less foreign to us than his writings on physics or psychology, and they are therefore both easier to read and easier to misunderstand without realizing it. In my treatment of these areas I have therefore decided not to attempt a detailed summary of the contents of the relevant works. I have sought instead to set forth the outlines of Aristotle's distinctive approach to these issues, and to do this in such a way that both what is strange and what is familiar in his viewpoint become apparent to the reader.

I have been guided throughout by the principle that the best exposition of a person's ideas is a sympathetic one. That, plus the desire for conciseness, has led me to omit almost all criticism of Aristotle from this work. Further, for the reader at whom this book is primarily aimed, the controversies surrounding the interpretation of particular points in Aristotle's philosophy represent nothing but a distraction. I have therefore included almost no reference to these. But you are hereby placed on notice that nearly everything I say here has been disputed by one interpreter or another. Nonetheless, I have tried not to stray too far from widely accepted views of Aristotle's thought, whenever they were at all defensible. Above all, I have sought to stick close to Aristotle's own text, as I understood it.

The greatest or at least most difficult task in a text for beginners is to strike the right balance between sophistication and accessibility. I must admit that I think most earlier introductions to Aristotle have erred in one direction or the other, at least with regard to the audience I am aiming at. And some have managed to err in both ways, using language too technical and examples too specialized for most people, while presenting Aristotle's ideas in such rough sketches or in so condensed and simplified a form as to be unrecognizable. I do not pretend to have achieved perfection in this regard. But I have tried to include enough of Aristotle's ideas to be of real help to the student who wants to understand things, rather than simply creating an unjustified sense of familiarity with his thought. I have also tried to spell out assumptions that philosophically sophisticated readers often take for granted, but which beginning students are quite unaware of. And I have insisted on careful explanation, even at great length, of doctrines and assumptions that are hard to understand and which, if misunderstood, lead to a quick dismissal of Aristotelian ideas.

Use of earlier versions of this work with undergraduates in a small liberal arts college suggests that I have been moderately successful in these aims. Of course, the only way to tell for sure whether a book will work for you is for you to read it. What I have said so far is only meant to help you decide whether it is worth making that trial.

I

Wisdom and Science

Etymologically speaking, the word "philosophy" means "the love of wisdom," and one way of approaching the thought of a philosopher is to investigate what he or she understands by "wisdom" and by "love." In Aristotle's case, "love" seems to refer simply to a kind of desire, so that the love of wisdom is just a desire to become wise, or a commitment to the pursuit of wisdom. The term "wisdom," however, is more problematic, and our survey can appropriately revolve around the attempt to explicate its meaning. This approach is quite in the spirit of Aristotle, for whom the goal or end of an activity, the thing at which it aims, is the key to understanding it.

Aristotle himself defines wisdom as "intuition and scientific knowledge of the most valuable things." We will proceed by explaining the various components of this definition, beginning with scientific knowledge.

"Scientific knowledge" is a translation of the term *episteme*. This is sometimes translated simply as "knowledge," sometimes simply as "science." However you translate it, it is supposed to signify something better than mere true belief about something. But what? We can say that to have scientific knowledge of a fact is to be able to give a scientific explanation of it. But what is a scientific explanation?

For Aristotle, to have scientific knowledge of a fact, it is not enough to know that it is true; you must also know *why* it is true. A scientific explanation states why the fact is so, and that is the same thing as stating the causes of the fact. As a general description, this probably agrees with the conception of science held by the average person today. But when we begin to get more specific about the meaning and implications of this description, Aristotle parts company with us. In particular, he has his own distinctive

11

conceptions of the kind of fact that can be scientifically explained, of the kinds of causes there are, and of the form in which a scientific explanation should be cast.

To show the causes of a fact is, in Aristotle's view, to show that the fact has to be the way it is, or as he prefers to put it, that it cannot be otherwise than it is. A fact that just happens to be true is not scientifically knowable; only a fact which is necessarily true can be known scientifically. A consequence of this is that particular truths about particular individuals cannot be objects of scientific knowledge. For no individual necessarily exists; if you or I had never been born, that would violate no law of nature, metaphysics, or logic. If you or I had not been born, then all the things that are now true about us would not have been true. Hence, all of those facts could be otherwise than they are. In modern terminology, all of the facts about individuals as individuals are contingent.

But what other kinds of facts are there? Facts about kinds of things, about species and genera. ("Genera" is the plural of "genus"; "species" is the same in the singular and the plural.) Aristotle's use of the terms "genus" and "species" is the basis of our modern biological use of the terms. But they were not quite as rigid in Aristotle's usage. In our system of classification, "genus" and "species" refer to two relatively specific categories near the bottom of each part of the system (or, if you draw the scheme of classification as a tree with the most general class at the bottom, then genus and species go near the outermost tips of the branches). "Genus" and "species" used to be the most specific categories, before we began to distinguish subspecies and varieties within a species. Above (more general than) genus and species, you recall, are things like phylum and family and so on. Aristotle didn't have such an elaborate scheme, or such a diverse terminology. He used "genus" and "species" for any two consecutive levels of generality. Hence, what is a genus relative to a lower class can be called a species relative to a higher one. He would say, for example, that human being is a species of primate and primate a species of mammal, or conversely, that mammal is the genus of primate and primate the genus of human being. (For convenience, I have used modern categories here; Aristotle didn't talk about "primates" and "mammals.") Another difference between Aristotle's usage and ours is that he didn't use "species" and "genus" only in biology.

He used them in every science.

To get back to the main point, then, since all of the facts about individuals as individuals are contingent, the proper object of scientific knowledge is facts about genera and species, or since any class except the very most general can be described as a species, we can just say, facts about species. Only facts about species qualify as scientifically knowable, because only they can be necessary. That all humans are rational is necessarily true. That Tim Robinson is rational is not necessarily true. Now it is true that, given that I am a human being, I must be rational. But that is only a hypothetical necessity: on the "hypothesis" or condition that I am human, it follows that I must be rational. My being rational is contingent on my being human. And my being human is not necessary, for the reasons outlined above. What we want for scientific knowledge is not facts which are hypothetically necessary, facts which depend for their existence on merely contingent circumstances, but facts which result from circumstances which are themselves necessary and therefore impart their own necessity to their effects.

This is perhaps a good place to clarify a peculiarity of Aristotle's language which occasions some confusion. Aristotle talks a lot about "substances." In modern English this term refers to a homogeneous "stuff," like water or air, or any of the chemical elements. But for Aristotle, a substance in the primary sense of the term (called for this reason a "first substance") was any individual entity: a horse, a dog, a human being, a chair. Don't be misled by language here. It is not the class of dogs, for example, that is a first substance; it is the particular, individual dog, this dog Fido, who is a first substance. It may help to remember this if you keep in mind that "substance" comes from the Latin *substantia*, which was a translation of the Greek *ousia*, and *ousia* means "being." A substance is primarily a being, and the things that most qualify as beings (for Aristotle) are particular individual entities. You and I count as first substances. Genus and species are referred to as "second substances"; the species human being can be called a being only in a secondary sense. The statement that only facts about species are scientifically knowable could be restated: Only facts about secondary substances are scientifically knowable.

Most of what Aristotle has to say about substances will be a lot clearer if you keep the previous paragraph in mind. But I should also warn you that there are places, particularly in his *Metaphysics*, where he wrestles with various meanings for the term, and in different passages he seems to favor different meanings as primary. Interpreters disagree over which passage represents Aristotle's final judgment on the matter. In the present exposition, anyway, I will continue to take particular individuals as the prime examples of substances.

You should now be able to understand why I said above that facts about individuals *as individuals* cannot be known scientifically. The phrase "as individuals" is crucial. That all humans are rational is a fact about you and me. But it is a fact about us as members of our species, not as individuals. You and I are rational as human beings, not as Tim and Sue and Jeff.

Incidentally, Aristotle got a lot of mileage out of that simple word "as." The Greek was *hei* (pronounced "hay"), which was translated into Latin as *qua*. The Latin term has been taken over into English, and most English dictionaries include it. *Webster's New World*, for example, defines it as "in the function, character, or capacity of," and illustrates it with "the President qua Commander in Chief." The term is used to designate the particular aspect of a thing with respect to which some assertion is made about it. Aspects may be distinguished on the basis of different levels of generality; for example, the human being qua human being is rational, but the human being qua animal is capable of sensation. But we can also distinguish aspects on the same level of generality. The bookcase as a colored object is brown, but qua massive object, it weighs forty pounds. Probably the best known Aristotelian use of the term is in his definition of metaphysics as "the science of being qua being." This rather mysterious-sounding phrase actually means something quite straightforward. Metaphysics seeks to explain what is true of everything which is, when considered solely with reference to the fact that it is, disregarding the characteristics which distinguish one kind of entity from another.

We can summarize our exposition so far by saying that the only facts which are scientifically knowable are necessary facts about species. Each science has a species as its subject matter. To know the facts about a species scientifically is to be able to demonstrate that those facts are necessary.

To avoid confusion about this, I should point out that not every organized body of knowledge is a science. Aristotle wrote treatises on logic, conceived not only as a tool for debate but also as an instrument for constructing sciences, but logic itself is not a science. Similarly, the knowledge of rhetoric, the art of persuasion, can be systematized, and Aristotle wrote on this, too, but this treatise does not demonstrate necessary facts about a species. There are yet other departments of knowledge which Aristotle will call sciences, but to which the description I have given does not readily apply. The subject of metaphysics is being, and being is treated like a species in some ways in that science, but strictly speaking, being is a peculiar sort of concept that represents neither a substance (either first or second) nor an attribute of a substance, and metaphysics ends up being a peculiar sort of science. The description I am giving here refers to sciences in the strictest and most fundamental sense of the term, and will apply to some of the things called sciences only in an extended or modified sense. It is the stricter sense of the term I have in mind when I say that having scientific knowledge means being able to demonstrate that certain facts about a species are necessary.

The circumstances that render a fact necessary are referred to as the "causes" of that fact. This brings us to another point of difference between Aristotle and modern conceptions of science. Aristotle uses the term "cause" in a very special sense, and the exposition of that sense must form a major portion of our discussion.

THE FOUR CAUSES

To understand Aristotle's conception of "cause," it helps to keep in mind that most of his explanations revolve around changes. Aristotle recognized four kinds of change: (1) motion, or change of place; (2) the coming to be or passing away of a thing (these are sometimes called "generation and corruption"), such as conception, death, the manufacture of a shoe or of a statue; (3) growth and diminution, like inflating a balloon or putting on weight (and their opposites); and (4) alteration in quality, such as getting warm or changing colors. We could sum it up in Aristotelian terminology by saying that changes occur in the categories of place, substance, quantity, and quality. Most explanations revolve around such processes, and even when you are trying to understand the constitution of an object rather than a change in it, you look at the genesis of the object, the changes to which it is subject, and the ways it behaves as clues to its constitution.

In modern usage, "cause" refers to an event or condition which brings about or facilitates the occurrence of another event or condition. This does not exactly correspond to Aristotle's usage. Aristotle's word for "cause" is *aitia*. In ordinary Greek, this can be used to refer to any sort of reason why something happens. (The corresponding adjective, *aitios*, means "responsible.") Aristotle uses "cause" for any of the factors which must be identified in giving a complete account of a change. He recognizes four varieties of that kind of thing, and these are his famous "four causes." They are most easily defined by means of an example.

Let's think about the sculpting of a statue. It will be easiest if we think of some particular sculptor producing some particular statue—although scientific knowledge is about species rather than individuals, it's okay to use an individual as an example to help clarify the meaning of a term. Another point about this example is that it involves an artistic process, and it isn't the same in every respect as a natural process. But after I've laid out the basic ideas, we can go on to complicate matters. Let's imagine a fairly straightforward, routine instance of sculpting: a second-rate sculptor known for producing workmanlike marbles of Civil War generals, city founders, and the like, is churning out another monument for somebody's home town. There are basically four things we want to notice in this process. The first and most conspicuous is the statue itself which results from it. To understand the process you must recognize it as aiming at (and hence naturally terminating in) the production of a statue, and more specifically, of a statue of a certain kind, and most specifically, of a particular statue of a particular person in a particular position. This is the end of the process, both in the sense of the place where it stops and in the sense of what it aimed at. Aristotle, too, calls it the *end*, or the *final cause*. At the opposite end of the process, we have the raw material from which the statue is made: marble, usually in a box-shaped block. In Aristotelian terminology, this is the *matter*, or the *material cause*. Comparing the matter and the end, we can ask ourselves, "What's the difference?" The difference is that the marble now, at the end, has the shape of the statue, the shape that makes it the statue it is. That characteristic by virtue of which the end is what it is, or more generally, that attribute by virtue of which any thing is what it is, Aristotle calls the *form* or the *formal cause* of the thing. The last factor we have to examine is the sculptor herself. She is the one responsible for that form's coming to be in that matter, and she did it by first conceiving that form in her head and then realizing it through the exercise of her artistic techniques. Aristotle will call her the *agent* or the *efficient cause* of the statue.

I have assumed in this example that the shape of a statue is what makes it the particular statue it is, and hence what makes it a particular kind of statue, and hence what makes it a statue at all. I make that assumption because it makes the example easier to grasp. Artists and theorists of art may disagree. In fact, even Aristotle would disagree, because art is more complicated than that. But I won't go into that now. (I discuss it more in the second section of the chapter on politics.) A more important point for present purposes is that you must not assume that "form" always means "shape." Shape is just one kind of form, and while some things are defined by their shapes, many are not. Generally, in describing a change, the form is whatever makes the product of the change the kind of thing it is; it's what the matter has after the change that it didn't have before it. When a leaf changes its color in the autumn, the new color is a form that defines the result of this change. If you warm your toes at a fire, your toes are acquiring the form "warmth." If you get angry, anger is the form you have acquired. And if you are standing still and then start walking, you have taken on the form of "walking." Note two things about this last example: First, the causes can be used to explain not just a static quality that a thing comes to have, but also an activity in which it is engaged; that too is a form. Second, when I say that the form is responsible for the thing's being the kind of thing it is, this must be taken in a very broad sense. Membership in a biological species (homo sapiens) or in an artificial kind (statue) is dictated by form, but so is membership in any other sort of class: In the example, you have gone from being a non-walking thing to being a walking thing. That represents the acquisition of a form.

The end, as you can see, is just the matter plus the form. It is the matter with the form imposed on it, the formed matter. In this example, the end can also be described as the aim or purpose of the process. But "end" and "purpose" are not synonymous. A purpose is only one kind of end. "Purpose" carries connotations of deliberation and choice, and hence is appropriate only to the actions of animals who are capable of deliberating and choosing. But the four causes can be found in every change, not just in the actions of intelligent beings. This is an important point, because some popularizers of Aristotle have overlooked it and consequently misinterpreted his natural philosophy. When he says, "Nature always acts for an end," they take that to mean that natural processes are guided by rational or intelligent purpose. It is true that he saw an order in the world which was no different from the order reason would have given it, if the world had been built by reason. But he doesn't draw the conclusion that there is some intelligent being responsible for it all. When he says that nature always acts for an end, all he means, at least in the simpler cases, is that for every natural process there is a point at which the process is complete and at which, accordingly, it naturally stops. Things get more complicated when we look not at a one-time event but at an ongoing process (like the revolutions of the planets), or at the functioning of a component within a larger system (like the pumping of the heart), but the basic idea remains the same. Most of the final causes in the universe are just results built into the processes that lead to them; they involve no element of conscious purpose.

When an action *is* purposive, we have to distinguish nearer and more remote purposes. On the principle that we should explain things by going from simple to complex, a change should always be explained in terms of its closest, or as Aristotelians say, "most proximate" end. The sculptor's ultimate purpose in making the statue may be to win fame and fortune, but that tells us little about the particular process of sculpting. We must first recognize the production of this statue as the proximate end of the sculpting and as the end appropriate to understanding sculpting in general. Later and in other contexts, we could examine the other, more remote ends which the sculptor may be pursuing. (The term "ulterior purpose," now used to describe a hidden and less reputable motive than the one publicly admitted, originally meant "a more remote purpose," a purpose beyond the one immediately belonging to the action; "ulterior" literally means "later" or "more final," just as "ultimate" means "last" or "final.")

In the coming to be of a statue, or in any process of production, the matter is the raw material. But in other changes, "raw material" is an inappropriate term. The matter is in every case what might be called the "subject" of the change. It is the thing which undergoes the change and is present throughout the process. It is the thing which comes to have a form it didn't have before, or trades one form for another. For instance, if the sculptor goes on to paint his statue, the matter in this second change is the statue itself. (Our statues are seldom painted, but it was quite common among Greek sculptors.) If you start walking (come to have the form of "walking"), you are the matter in this process.

If the sculptor paints his statue, I said, the matter in this change is the statue itself. Notice how what is the end relative to one process (sculpting) can become the matter for another (painting). Indeed, this was already illustrated by the sculpting example itself, inasmuch as the block of marble with which the sculptor begins is the product of a process of geological metamorphosis; the sculptor's matter is the final cause of that geological process. The upshot of it is that things can play different roles in different changes, so that whether a thing is matter, form, agent, or end is relative to a particular change.

The agent of a change is the thing which initiates the change, the thing which causes the motion to begin, the mover. As the sculptor example illustrates, the agent is what brings it about that the matter possesses a certain form. This form which the matter is to acquire must pre-exist in some manner in the agent, though its mode of existence in the agent can be quite different from its eventual mode of existence in the matter which undergoes the change. The form of the statue as it exists in the sculptor's mind or, as Aristotle prefers to say, in the sculptor's art, is different from the form embodied in the statue. But it is also in a way the same.

Let's look at some more examples. Suppose a blacksmith puts a piece of iron in the forge to heat it up. We won't examine the blacksmith's act of placing the iron in the forge, but just the process of heating which subsequently takes place. What are the four causes in this process? The end is that the iron is hot: hot piece of iron. The matter is the iron, which was first cold and then hot. The form is the heat which the iron comes to have. The agent is the fire.

Here's an example in which the causes are a little harder to distinguish. Suppose I drop my pen. Just as, in the previous example, we ignored the blacksmith's putting the iron in the forge to concentrate on the process of heating, so in this case let's forget about

my clumsiness in losing my grip on the pen and just focus on the
pen's falling to earth. We explain this by reference to the force of
gravity, but how would Aristotle explain it? We have to remember
that our conception of the force of gravity is part of a physical
theory first proposed by Sir Isaac Newton some 2000 years after
Aristotle's death. Before then, "gravity" was a synonym for
"heaviness" or "weight"; it was a property of a heavy thing, rather
than a force of attraction that existed between things. In this frame
of reference, gravity can be described as the power a thing has to
move itself downwards when support is removed from it.
Aristotle, of course, thought that the earth was at the center of the
cosmos, and that the universe was organized in concentric circles
around it. Hence, for him, the effect of gravity is to move a thing
toward the center of the universe.

Now where are the four causes in the falling of a pen? If the pen
is "trying" to get to the center of the cosmos, then that is the place
where its motion would naturally cease. The final cause or end, in
other words, is that the pen should be located at the center. If pen-
at-the-center is the final cause, then the formal cause is the one
that defines that end, namely location at the center, being at the
center. What is the matter? The thing which undergoes the change
in this instance is just the pen itself; that is the matter. So far, so
good. But where is the agent cause? The agent or efficient cause,
we said, was the "mover," the thing that brings about the motion.
In the case of the statue, this was the sculptor, or more accurately,
it was the sculpting activity of the sculptor. But in the case of
the pen falling, there is no one and nothing outside the pen
which makes it fall. As we said above, the pen's "gravity" (in the
pre-Newtonian sense of the term) is precisely its ability to move
itself. The agent of this motion is not separate from the thing
moved. Aristotle would insist that mover and moved are not
identical, for a thing cannot be mover and moved in the same
sense at the same time. But the mover in this instance is somehow
internal to the moved. This is the difference between natural and
artificial processes. In all artificial processes, the agent cause is
external to the thing moved; in all natural processes, the agent is
internal. In fact, this internal agent cause is precisely what
Aristotle calls "nature."

We will have to talk at greater length about nature. The discussion of causality provides us with the necessary background for

explaining that and several other key terms of Aristotelian science. But before we turn to that, I'd like to do two things: first, to point out one important consequence of Aristotle's conception of causality, and second, to summarize some guidelines for identifying the four causes in any instance of change.

Aristotle made a claim that is sometimes expressed by saying that cause and effect must exist simultaneously. You should now be in a position to see why and in what sense he believed that. In every change, which is to say, in every instance of causation, there is an active element and a passive element. The former is the agent; the latter is the matter. The cause (specifically, the efficient cause) of the change is the action or activity of the agent. The effect, the change itself, takes place in the matter. The effect is the being-acted-upon of the matter. Aristotle says that the action of the agent and the being-acted-upon of the matter must occur at the same time. And this makes perfectly good sense. The activity of the sculptor making the statue and the "passivity" of the statue being made are simultaneous aspects of one and the same process. I bring this up because it is on this point that the contrast is sharpest between the Aristotelian and the modern conceptions of causality. If you think of a cause as an event which brings about or conditions a subsequent event, then by definition, cause and effect cannot be simultaneous. And once you have separated cause and effect into different (even if immediately successive) times, you are open to all sorts of questions about the necessity of the connection between them. How can the content of one moment determine the content of the next moment? And even if it can, how could we ever be sure that it did? I won't go into this any further, but if you study modern philosophy, particularly the philosophy of David Hume, you will see what tremendous ramifications this interpretation of causality has.

I will conclude this section with some guidelines for identifying the four causes in any particular instance of change:

1. The first cause to try to identify is the end. Do this by asking, Where does this process naturally terminate? What is the result of the change? Remember that the result is described by reference to its form, but the end includes both the form and the matter. Look for the immediate, "most proximate" end, not more remote ends.

2. Seek the form by asking, What characteristics distinguish the end from the beginning? That is, what characteristics distinguish how the matter was before the change from how it is after the change? The process is the kind of process it is because it has a particular kind of result: sculpting is sculpting because it produces a three-dimensional artwork—that's what sculpting is. If you know what kind of process you're looking at, then you know the form of the result. Sometimes the process is named after the form of the result. Heating is the process that results in something's being hot.

3. Identify the matter by asking, What received the form, what is it that underwent this change, what was there before the change took place and still there (but with a different form) at the end of it? What was the end before it had this form?

4. What brought about the process? What initiated the change? What had the form in some way or other before the change took place and through this process produced this form in this matter? That's the agent.

The Vocabulary of Science

So far, we have been working with a definition of science as knowledge of the causes of things. But we could equally well describe science as knowledge of the natures of things. These definitions are not quite synonymous, but they are nearly so—if you understand the second definition as Aristotle would. To see this, we must explain Aristotle's conception of *nature*.

Of all the modern uses of the word "nature," the one that comes closest to the Aristotelian sense is the one illustrated by the phrase "the nature of a thing." Aristotle does not use "nature" to refer to the universe, or to the world as it exists or would exist apart from human interference. Much less does he use it for some force, presence, or deity which oversees all things or all nonhuman things (as when we talk about "Mother Nature"). He does at times say things that sound like this, so there's room for debate on this point. But in general, I think he would be most comfortable with the way we use "the nature of a thing" to refer to the attributes which a thing necessarily possesses because of the kind of thing it is. He would be even happier when we use this phrase to focus on the behavior of a thing, on what it does or how it acts on other things. ("Why do people do such-and-such?" "It's just human nature.") Aristotle's usage of "nature" is closely tied to this notion of the way a thing behaves because of the kind of thing it is. But we must go a little further than this to grasp his precise meaning.

For Aristotle, the nature of a thing is not the way it behaves but the cause of its behaving in this way. But now that you have learned about the four causes, your immediate response to this statement will be to ask, Which kind of cause are you talking about?

The simplest answer is to say that it is the agent cause we are referring to here. Think again about me dropping my pen. The heaviness of the pen is nothing more than its power of moving itself toward the center of the world. The efficient cause of this motion is that in the pen which moves it in this way. As we said above, the agent is "somehow internal" to the thing moved. This is precisely what Aristotle means by the nature of a thing: it is *an agent cause internal to the thing moved.* The contrast we drew earlier between the falling of a pen and the production of a statue is the distinction Aristotle would make in general between natural processes and the processes of art. He used "art" not just for the fine arts, but for any human productive activity. In the arts, so defined, the moving cause is separate from the thing moved, the producer separate from the product. In natural motion, no such separation is possible.

There is ample room for confusion here, so let's be careful. The above description applies to what might be called the paradigm cases of natural as opposed to artificial changes. In other cases it will be more complicated.

Let's stick with the falling pen for a minute. What I have said so far might lead you to believe that Aristotle would accept the statment that it's in the nature of the pen to fall. He wouldn't think that was flat wrong, but he would regard it as misleading. The pen's falling is natural. But remember that the nature of a thing is the cause of its behaving the way it does because of the kind of thing it is. And every thing in the world is several kinds of thing at the same time. This pen is also red. But it would be misleading to say, "It's in the nature of this red object to fall." Statements about natural motions should be tied to that aspect of a thing that the

motion is strictly associated with, not to other aspects only incidentally associated with the motion. Aristotle would say that the
pen falls not because it is red, nor because it is a pen, but because
it is made predominantly of "earthy" matter. In place of our 103
elements, Aristotle recognized only four: earth, air, fire, and water
(these were all the elements in our neighborhood of the cosmos;
when doing astronomy, he added another one he called "aether"
as the matter of the heavenly bodies). The various kinds of basic
solid substances were just so many varieties of earth. And some
solid substances included elements other than earth in their composition. Wood, for example, obviously contains some water because it gives off water when it burns.

To get back to gravity: The downward motion we associate with
gravity was a property of earth and of all the species of earth, and
hence is also a property of every object in which earthy matter is
the predominant ingredient. Hence, "It's in the nature of earthy
matter to fall" is strictly true. When my pen falls, the fact that it is
a pen has no role to play in explaining its motion. Its being a pen is
incidental, or as Aristotelians would say, "accidental" to the fact of
its falling. By contrast, when I am using the pen to write, its being
a pen is not accidental to this use—that's what pens are made for,
and to be a pen is to be an instrument for writing. When I'm writing, the essential thing about the pen is that it's a pen; when the
pen is falling, the essential thing is that it's made of earth. You
might sum it up by saying that to speak accurately about natures
and causes, you have to make sure you're working on the right
level of analysis.

This is a place where the term "qua," introduced earlier, comes
in handy. You will recall that this term is used to isolate the aspect
of a thing which is relevant to a particular assertion about it. The
point of the previous paragraph could be restated thus: It is not in
the nature of the pen qua pen to fall, but it is in the nature of the
pen qua earthy object.

Aristotle thought that each of his four elements had its natural
place in the cosmos, its level to which it naturally moved. Earth is
naturally on bottom, water above that, air above that, and fire on
top. That's why flames leap upward. Each of these elements has a
nature, and the nature of each is to move to its proper place. Our
region of the universe hasn't become nicely stratified because the
rotation of the spheres out of which the universe is constructed,

and the processes that result from that rotation (the cycle of the seasons, with everything that depends on that) keep the elements stirred up.

Aristotle referred to earth, air, fire, and water as "elements" because he thought they were as simple as things ever get. There were no more basic constituents into which they could be analyzed. He did believe that these elements were capable of being changed into each other. Or to be more exact, he thought you could take a batch of, say, earth and change it into fire—this is part of what's happening when wood burns. He believed that in such changes there must be some constant matter that underwent the change, that traded one set of qualities for another—his analysis of the four causes required such a thing. But since the qualities in question were supposed to be most basic, not reducible to more primitive qualities, the matter that underlies these changes must be supposed to have no qualities of its own at all. This qualityless and hence formless matter Aristotle called "prime matter." One of the important things to remember about prime matter is that you will never find it anywhere on its own, in isolation from any attributes. Everything that is real has some characteristics, and that means that everything that is real has some form. Prime matter is simply postulated as the source of continuity in changes from one most basic form to another.

Prime matter sounds so much like nothing at all that some recent interpreters have argued that Aristotle didn't really believe in it. Others have held that he did, but that doing so was inconsistent with other things he believed. The jury is still out on this one. The view presented above represents the traditional interpretation.

Some further discussion of the elements will help us get clearer about the meaning of "nature" and about the relationship between "nature" and "form." To call earth an element is to imply that it cannot be broken down into simpler constituents. It does have a plurality of qualities—it is cold and dry, as well as heavy. And these qualities, as its form, can be distinguished from the prime matter on which this form is imposed. But though it can be "divided" in these ways, it is still elemental in the sense that none of these parts is a substance with qualities of its own. Earth cannot be analyzed into parts with more basic qualities or powers which are responsible for the qualities or powers that earth itself has. In the case of things which are composite, their attributes can often be explained as functions of the attributes of their components. You can explain the operation of a motor, for example, by talking about the operation of the simpler devices that form its parts: levers, gears, pistons, and so on. You can explain the workings of the eye by talking about the various mechanisms by which light waves are focused on the retina and translated into patterns of neuron firings. But this kind of analysis cannot be done on an element. (The fact that it can be done on what *we* call elements just shows that they aren't really elements; they are treated like elements for certain kinds of chemistry, but for others they must be analyzed into the more elemental protons, neutrons, and electrons. And for atomic physicists, the analysis must be carried even further.) The attributes of an element cannot be explained in terms of the attributes of more elemental parts, which means they cannot be explained (accounted for causally) at all. All we can say about the attributes of an element is, that's the way it is. This kind of thing has these attributes, because to have these attributes is what it means to be this kind of thing, and that's the end of it. The nature of an elemental substance, therefore, simply is its power to operate in a certain way. The heaviness of earth, as one of its natural properties, simply is its power to move itself toward the center, and that power is an integral aspect of its form. Consequently, to describe the nature of a simple object or kind of object is simply to inventory its powers, to take stock of the ways it behaves. In such cases, that is also how you would describe the form of the object, so we may say that for elemental or simple objects, form and nature are identical. (And both must be explicated in terms of the end.)

It might seem that form and nature are identical in all natural objects, whether simple or not. A natural object, or as Aristotle sometimes puts it, a thing that exists by nature, is a thing that moves itself. To be a thing of a certain kind is to have the power of moving or changing in a certain way. Hence, to be a natural object is to have within oneself a particular kind of agent cause. Since the formal cause is what makes a thing the particular kind of thing it is, the form of a natural object can be identified with the agent cause inherent in it.

This conclusion is acceptable within the boundaries of a science, where we are talking about species rather than individuals. To identify the form of a species, say, "human being," is to say what is characteristic of every human being qua human being. And for Aristotle, that means to identify the distinctively human activity. That distinctive activity, again in Aristotle's view, is the use of our cognitive powers in reasoning, constructing sciences, deliberating courses of action, and communicating with other humans. The human being is therefore defined as the rational animal. And this definition states both the form of human being and the nature of the human being.

In the case of an individual rather than a species, to equate form with nature is to invite confusion. Every attribute of an individual can be considered a part or aspect of its form. But to speak of the nature of an individual is to speak of those characteristics that make the individual a certain kind of thing, characteristics that the individual shares with other members of the same species. In the individual then, nature is only part of the form.

In the case of elements and other simple objects, the form of a kind of thing cannot be described otherwise than by describing its behaviors, actions, or effects. But in complex objects, as I indicated above, one can go further. Consider once again my pen. This, of course, is not a natural object, but it might make the point more clearly for all that. In the case of artifacts, we speak of their functions rather than of their behaviors. The function of a pen is quite clear. It is an instrument for writing; its function is to write. If it could be said to have a nature, its nature would be the power of writing. This would also be its form. But in this case, the form can be analyzed further. For the form of the pen—the set of qualities by virtue of which it is a pen—is complex, and we can describe this complexity. To be specific, it is a pen because of its design, because of the way it is put together. We can draw a picture to show the individual components of the pen and how they are put together. This is to describe the form of the pen in detail. But it is because of this design that the pen is capable of fulfilling its function. Hence, to analyze the form of the pen is also to analyze the "agent cause" of its functioning. Keep in mind that this is really just an analogy. The pen doesn't move itself, so it doesn't really have an agent cause as a pen. But if it did, you would describe it by describing the design that enables it to fulfill its end.

In simple objects, form is the power of acting in a certain way. In complex objects, form is in many cases to be identified with the design of the object which enables it to act in a certain way. There are also other meanings for "form," which we will discuss when we turn to Aristotle's conception of the soul. In all of these senses, the form of a natural object can be identified with its nature, and the form of an artificial object with the function it is meant to perform. This is not to say that having a certain design, for example, means the same thing as functioning in a certain way, but that the design is responsible for the thing's ability to function in that way. Also, remember that the context in which we are equating form with nature or function is one in which we are speaking about species rather than individuals. In fact, "form" and "species" are translations of the same Greek word.

In the light of the preceding exposition, we can very briefly define several other technical terms of Aristotle's.

The attributes that belong to a thing by virtue of its being the kind of thing it is are referred to as its "essential attributes." They belong to every thing of that kind, and do so necessarily. For they are responsible for the thing's being what it is; if one of them were missing, it would be a different kind of thing.

Among the essential attributes of a thing, some are more "central" than others. What I mean by this is that the possession of some of them can be shown to follow from the possession of others. Another way of putting this is to say that the possession of some of these attributes is the cause—the formal cause—of the possession of others. The attributes from which the other attributes follow are said to constitute the "essence," in the strict sense, of that kind of thing. The essence of a thing is what the thing is. To identify the essence of a thing is to state what it is, to give a definition of it (Aristotle sometimes refers to a definition as "the formula of the essence"). Whatever other attributes belong necessarily and essentially to a thing belong to it because it is that kind of thing.

An example may help clarify the relationship between "essence" and "essential attribute." A triangle may be defined as a closed rectilinear plane figure having three sides. This definition names certain essential attributes of triangles, and it states the essence of a triangle. Within the framework of Euclidean geometry, you can prove that the internal angles of a triangle are equal to two right angles. This is also an essential attribute of a triangle, but it is not part of the essence. The essence consists of just those attributes named in the definition; other attributes which follow from these are also essential, but not part of the essence.

The attributes definitive of a kind of thing, or species (that is, those which constitute the essence of the kind), can be grouped into (a) those which locate this species in a more comprehensive genus, and (b) the property which distinguishes this species from the others in that genus. This is why Aristotelian definitions are said to consist of genus and difference, or sometimes "genus and specific difference." The idea that a definition consists of genus and species is not Aristotelian, for in Aristotle's framework, the species is the thing being defined.

The attribute which distinguishes one species from another in the same genus must be a property of that species. The term "property" has a very special sense in Aristotle. A property is an essential attribute, and therefore belongs to every member of a species. But in addition, a property belongs exclusively to members of that species. For example, if the human being can be defined as the rational animal, then rationality, as the property which provides the specific difference for humans, must belong to all humans and it must belong only to humans. If members of some other species in another genus exhibit something like rationality, it can only be "like" human rationality. The difference of genera forces it to be something different. And if it should turn out that some other species within the same genus (animal) exhibits rationality, that means that rationality is not a property of humans and does not serve to distinguish our species from that other one. That, in turn, means that our definition is ill-formed, and we'll have to try again.

Since to be a natural object of a certain kind is to have the power of moving or changing in a characteristic way, to define a kind of natural object, to state its essence, is to identify those aspects of its form which are responsible for its behaving in this characteristic way. Its essence is its nature.

At this point we can offer a revised definition of science which integrates the main points of the preceding discussion. To have scientific knowledge is to be able to give a scientific explanation of a fact. The subject matter of a science is a set of facts about a species. Each of these facts consists in the possession of some attribute by that species. To explain such a fact is to show that the attribute in question belongs necessarily to that species. A scientific explanation does this by defining the species (stating its essence) and demonstrating that the possession of the attribute in question necessarily follows from this definition. To do this is simultaneously to demonstrate the cause of the species' possessing this attribute.

We've one thing left to do to round out our picture of Aristotelian science: to explore the forms of language in which scientific eplanations must be cast.

THE FORM OF SCIENTIFIC EXPLANATION

Aristotle was perhaps the first person to notice that in many of the explanations we give, the logical relationships among the parts of the explanation are the same as the logical relationships among the parts of an argument. We might abbreviate that by saying that explanation has the form of argument. This is not immediately obvious. Explaining why something is so and proving that something is so are certainly two different things. It helps a little to keep in mind Aristotle's own conception of scientific explanation, in which it is the concern of science not to prove that something is so, but to show that some admitted fact is necessary. Explaining why something is so and showing that it is necessarily so don't sound so far apart. And showing that something is necessarily so doesn't sound so very different from proving it. But to see how all of these things can be said to have the same form, we have to be more explicit about what that form is.

The heart of a scientific explanation, in Aristotle's view, was something he called a "demonstration." I have been using this word for some time in this exposition, but now I must announce that it is a very special technical term in Aristotle, with a well-defined meaning. We can begin our account of this meaning by saying that a demonstration is an argument. And we'd best dwell on this idea for a moment.

For most purposes, an argument can be defined as a series of statements consisting of (a) a conclusion which the arguer wants you to believe, or to believe in more strongly, or to regard as more probable or as more certainly true than you did before, and (b) one or more premises meant to bring about this result by stating evidence for that conclusion. Arguments can be constructed in various ways, and one of the most important variables in such structures is what might be called the "tightness of fit" between premises and conclusion. In less metaphorical terms, arguments differ in how strictly the conclusion follows from the premises. Some are so constructed that if the premises are true, the conclusion has to be true. In others, if the premises are true, it is more or less likely that the conclusion will be true. And in still others, the premises don't really give evidence for the conclusion at all; they just seem to. Obviously, the first of these possibilities represents the ultimate in argument strength. It defines the logician's ideal. And any argument which satisfies that ideal is said to be "valid." Validity can be defined more precisely as follows: An argument is valid when it is so constructed that the conclusion follows strictly from the premises—that is, it is so constructed that if the premises are all true, the conclusion must be true (it is strictly and logically impossible for the conclusion to be false).

A demonstration is not just any old argument. It has to be a valid argument. And even that isn't enough to define a demonstration. But before we see what else is needed, let's talk about Aristotle's way of dealing with what we've got so far.

Aristotle wrote six treatises on what he called "logic." The first three of these and the last one deal with what we nowadays call logic. The fourth and fifth treat the use of logic in science and in dialectic (and I'll explain later what dialectic is). The entire set is commonly referred to as the *Organon*. "Organon" is the Greek word for "tool," and this title expresses the idea that these six treatises provide the logical tools for scientific work (and for rational discussion in general).

The first treatise is called the *Categories*. In this work, Aristotle comes up with a classification of words—the smallest meaningful units of language—according to the kinds of things they refer to. The categories he identifies, with some examples of the words in each, are

Substance:	"a human being," "a horse"
Quantity:	"three feet long," "twenty gallons"
Quality:	"green," "learned," "strong," "hot"
Relation:	"double," "half"
Place:	"downtown," "at school"
Time:	"yesterday," "last year"
Position:	"is lying down," "is sitting"

Having:	"is shod," "is armed"
Acting:	"cuts," "burns"
Being acted upon:	"is cut," "is burned"

Besides identifying these categories, Aristotle discusses the logical properties of the words in each one—for example, the fact that a substance doesn't have an opposite (What is the opposite of a horse?) or that most qualities admit of variations in degree. He also distinguishes various meanings for several important terms, like "opposite," "prior," and "motion."

The second treatise of the *Organon* is usually called *On Interpretation*, but at least one translator entitles it *Propositions*, and that's a more accurate reflection of its content. It's about the sentences we make by combining two words to make an assertion. In other words, whereas the *Categories* looks at the simplest units of language, *On Interpretation* deals with the next higher level of complexity, which consists of the simplest sentences. Aristotle is interested only in declarative sentences, not in questions or imperatives. That's because he's not writing a general account of language, he's just gearing up to analyze arguments, in which only declarative sentences play a role. Much of the treatise is devoted to the logical relations among sentences of the forms "All A is B," "No A is B," "Some A are B," and "Some A are not B." (Notice that words like "all" and "is" didn't count as terms in the proposition; all of these examples would be described as propositions of two terms. Medieval logicians distinguished the two types of words as "categorematic"—the ones that count and that fit into the categories—and "syncategorematic"—the logical operators, like "some," "all," and "not." It's useful to have labels for these, but the medieval terminology has fallen out of use, I suppose because the words are so awkward.)

With two terms—not just any two, but an appropriate pair—you can construct a sentence. If you've got three (with the same qualification), you can make an argument. And that's the topic of the third treatise.

The third treatise is the *Prior Analytics*. It is called that because the third and fourth treatises were at first referred to together simply as the *Analytics*, and then distinguished as the earlier one and the later one. Hence, the fourth is called the *Posterior Analytics*.

The simplest form of argument is one constructed out of three terms. Any argument more complex than that should be reducible to a combination of three-term arguments. Another word for a three-term argument is "syllogism." The logicians' standard example of a syllogism is

All human beings are mortal.

Socrates is a human being.

Therefore, Socrates is mortal.

This is not perhaps the best example, because most syllogisms deal with classes rather than individuals, and Aristotelian science in particular never deals with individuals. But in any case, the important thing for logical purposes is the form of the syllogism, which in this case could be schematized as

All B are C.

All A are B.

Therefore, all A are C.

It may seem odd to read "Socrates is a human being" as "All A are B." But it is all of Socrates that is being placed in the class of "human being," and for that reason "Socrates is a human being" is not different in logical form from "All human beings are mortal." (This is true of Aristotelian logic, but modern symbolic logic gives these two statements radically different forms.)

The varieties of syllogism are distinguished by the arrangement of categorial terms and other words. Some of these arrangements yield valid syllogisms; others do not. The main aim of the *Prior Analytics* is to identify those forms of the syllogism which are valid.

The form just schematized is valid. It is by no means the only valid form of syllogism, but it is Aristotle's favorite. That's because it's the one that best illustrates the structure of scientific explanation. In a moment, I'll explain how that is so, but first let's take stock of how far we've got in defining "demonstration." A demonstration is an argument. It is a valid argument. And it is, more specifically, a valid syllogism.

But our definition is not yet complete, because not every valid syllogism is a demonstration. Demonstrations are distinguished from other valid syllogisms by the character of their premises. Discussing this will take us beyond questions of logical form. But before we take that step, we are already in a position to see how the logical form of a valid syllogism is also the form of a typical basic explanation of a fact.

The simplest facts there are consist in the possession of an attribute by a subject or a class of subjects. Such facts are stated by sentences of the form, "A is B" or "All A are B." To know the cause of such a fact is to know why the attribute B belongs to A. It is thus to know what links B to A, what is, so to speak, in the middle between them, binding them to each other.

Let's take a simple example. It is a fact that if you look at something through a convex lens (the type of lens in a magnifying glass), the thing looks bigger than when you look at it with the naked eye. This fact may not look like it fits the form "A is B," but if you think about it, it can also be expressed as, "A convex lens is a thing which makes things look bigger"; or even more simply, "A convex lens is a magnifier." (Notice that this means that *all* convex lenses are magnifiers; in ordinary speech we often omit the quantifying term.) We learn this fact from experience. But what is the reason for this fact? Why do convex lenses magnify? Most of us somewhere along the line picked up the idea that it has to do with the way light is refracted when it passes through the lens. We can't give a very sophisticated explanation in terms of the laws of optics or anything, but we basically understand that the lens concentrates the light passing through it into a smaller area. I don't know if a physicist would be satisfied with that explanation, but it will do for our purposes.

So here's our explanation: a convex lens magnifies because it concentrates light into a smaller area. In giving this explanation of the first fact, we have adduced a second fact. This second fact can also be put into the form "A is B." "A convex lens is a light-concentrator." We can thus write out our explanation in this way:

A convex lens is a light-concentrator.

That's why a convex lens is a magnifier.

But why does the first sentence explain the second? How does something's being a light-concentrator account for its being a magnifier? This question could be a request for a more detailed explanation of what's going on when you look through a magnifying glass, but that's not what I'm after here. You wouldn't even ask for a more detailed explanation unless the less detailed account at least qualified as a potential explanation. And it does that only if we make an additional assumption. A thing's being a light-concentrator would not explain its being a magnifier unless everything that is a light-concentrator is a magnifier. Consider, by contrast, the following "explanation":

A convex lens is a piece of glass.

That's why a convex lens is a magnifier.

We won't even consider this as a potential explanation, because we know that not every piece of glass is a magnifier. We know that "Every piece of glass is a magnifier" is not true. Accordingly, if we do even provisionally accept the earlier explanation, it's because we are prepared to accept the proposition that every light-concentrator is a magnifier.

So the complete explanation (the one with our assumption made explicit) runs like this:

Every light-concentrator is a magnifier.

A convex lens is a light-concentrator.

And that's why a convex lens is a magnifier.

If you now replace "and that's why" with "therefore," you have a syllogism; and its form is the one of which I said earlier that it best illustrates the form of scientific explanation:

All B is C:	Every light-concentrator is a magnifier.
All A is B:	A (implicitly, every) convex lens is a light-concentrator.
Therefore, all A is C:	A (implicitly, every) convex lens is a magnifier.

The fact that "and that's why" in the explanation can be replaced with "therefore" in the argument shows how a syllogism in the domain of logic reflects the situation of causality out there in

the world. Aristotle would maintain that every scientific explanation can be analyzed in a similar manner.

I said earlier that to know the cause of a fact is to know what
links that attribute to that subject. What this means is made evident by casting the explanation in syllogistic form. The link between being a convex lens and being a magnifier is being a light
concentrator. The cause occurs in the syllogism as the middle term
between the subject of the fact to be explained (which is also the
subject of the second premise) and the attribute (which is also the
predicate of the first premise). The scientist's search for causes is
precisely a search for such middle terms to fit into syllogisms. It is
success in this search which enables one to give a scientific explanation.

But valid syllogistic form is not enough to make an explanation
truly scientific. For that to happen, the premises of the syllogism
must also be of a certain sort. Here we turn to the final component
of our definition of "demonstration." In the *Posterior Analytics* (I, 2,
71b10 ff.), Aristotle lists and discusses six properties the premises
must have if a syllogism is to qualify as a demonstration. I'm going
to reduce that list to two.

First, remember that the point of a demonstration is to show
that the fact stated in the conclusion is necessary. To do this, we
must show that there are premises from which the fact strictly follows, or in other words, follows necessarily. This requirement is
fulfilled by constructing a valid argument. But this is not enough.
For this by itself only gives the fact a conditional or hypothetical
necessity; it is necessary on the assumption that the premises
are true. But what we want is an unconditional necessity. To get
that, we must build our argument out of premises that are themselves unconditionally necessary. In other words, we show the fact
to be unconditionally necessary by deducing it from unconditionally necessary premises in accord with rules of inference or argument forms which preserve necessity from premise to conclusion.
(The rules of validity do this.)

The traditional example of this kind of proof was the derivation
of a theorem of geometry from the axioms of geometry. In modern
times, it has been recognized that not all of the axioms of Euclidean geometry are logically necessary. And that raises the question
whether the modern conception of logical necessity corresponds
to the kind of necessity Euclid thought his axioms had, or to the

kind Aristotle thought the premises of a demonstration must have. And I suppose there's also room for debate about whether Aristotle and Euclid were on the same wave-length on this issue. These are issues I won't try to settle here. If you've studied geometry at all, you know what it's like to construct a proof, and you have a sense of what it would mean to look at an axiom and say, "Of course, that has to be true." Keeping that experience in mind will make what Aristotle says about demonstration seem more familiar.

To get a necessary conclusion, you must infer it from necessary premises. But how do we know that a premise is necessary? We can know this in either of two ways. We can turn a premise into a conclusion to be proven, and then find other necessary premises from which it necessarily follows. Or a premise can just be "self-evident." This is not Aristotle's term, but I think it is faithful to Aristotle's meaning. To call a premise self-evident is to say that one needs no evidence for it, apart from itself. In the simplest case, this happens because to *understand* the premise is immediately to see that it has to be true, to see that it could not possibly be false. A statement like "a = a," or "If a = b and b = c, then a = c" is supposed to be self-evident in this sense. Likewise for the law of noncontradiction, which in Aristotelian language could be expressed, "It is impossible for the same attribute both to belong and not to belong to the same subject at the same time and in the same respect." Anything which we say is true "by definition" should also qualify as self-evident. "Every married person has a spouse," "Illiterate people don't read newspapers," and (in Aristotle's view) "All human beings are rational" are self-evident in this sense.

To call something self-evident is not to say that its truth is immediately evident to anybody whatsoever. "A = A" means nothing to a newborn infant, and the law of noncontradiction that I quoted above can sound like gobbledygook to a person of considerable years. For many of us, the Pythagorean theorem is just something to be taken on faith—our math teachers wouldn't lie to us, would they? But for those who have done the proof, its truth is obvious in a way that it isn't for most of us. Most of us stand in the same relation to the Pythagorean theorem that little kids occupy with respect to the law of noncontradiction. The point is, it may take some doing to reach the point where you can understand a self-evident proposition. And if you are the first person to discover a particular self-evident proposition, it may take considerable cogitation before you can formulate and really comprehend that truth. It has to "dawn on you" that a self-evident proposition is true. Until that happens, the proposition may be evident in itself, but it isn't evident to you.

In the simplest cases, a proposition's becoming evident to you coincides with your achieving a genuine grasp of its meaning. In other cases, something more seems to be involved. I said earlier that a proposition is self-evident when one needs no evidence for it other than itself. It would seem, then, that a necessary truth is either self-evident or can be proven, but not both. But this conclusion must be qualified, and here again the Pythagorean theorem serves as a good illustration. Since you can construct a proof of the Pythagorean theorem, deriving it from the fundamental axioms of geometry, it would seem that we accept this proposition on the basis of this other evidence. And yet a geometer might claim that its truth is obvious. I think something for which there is a proof can be called "self-evident" in either of two senses. First, the expert geometer is so familiar with the proof of the theorem that he or she can be said to take in at one sweep the whole series of links between axioms and theorem. In effect, when confronted with the theorem, he or she can "just see" how it must follow from the axioms. The second possibility is when something strikes us as obviously and necessarily true, and we don't see any way that it could be derived from more basic truths. And then later, someone comes along and presents a proof of it. Until the proof came along, we would regard the proposition as self-evident in the strictest sense of the term. Afterwards, it could be self-evident only in the previously mentioned sense that we could take in the proof at one sweep.

Sciences are supposed to be founded ultimately on principles that are self-evident in what I just called the strictest sense of the term. When a proposition is self-evident in this sense, it can be used as a basis for proving other propositions, but there are no logically prior propositions that could be used to prove it. Such a principle is like an axiom that can only be an axiom; it cannot be turned into a theorem to be deduced from other axioms. In Aristotelian language, it is indemonstrable. Again, this is how we non-mathematicians think of the axioms of geometry. Recognizing the truth of this kind of principle seems to involve something more than simply grasping its meaning. But in this case, the "something more" is not seeing at a glance how the principle follows from prior principles, since there aren't any. What you can get in the case of a first principle is a sudden insight into its potential precisely to serve as a first principle, its potential, when conjoined with other first principles, to explain a wide range of phenomena or to enable you to deduce a broad system of theorems. In effect, you are realizing how all the disparate facts of a particular science fall into place when viewed in the light of these principles. One might argue that seeing what you can explain with a principle is part of what it means to understand its meaning. But this is certainly more complicated than recognizing the truth of something like "Every married person has a spouse." There we seem to be able to talk about self-evidence just in terms of grasping the meanings of the words in the sentence. There is no awareness of a lot of other propositions floating around in the background that will suddenly be reduced to order by recognizing the truth of this one. But that additional background is precisely what we do have in the case of scientific principles. Our awareness of the explanatory power of a principle forms a large part of our reasons for accepting it, and thus seems to be part of what we have in mind when we say that a principle is self-evident.

Our definition of "demonstration" is now complete. We had already established that every demonstration is a valid syllogism. We now add that for a valid syllogism to be a demonstration, its premises must be necessary, and they must either be self-evident in the strictest sense of the term, or they must be derivable by valid syllogisms from other propositions which are self-evident in the strictest sense. The criteria of necessity and self-evidence are not unrelated, for we have defined self-evidence in such a way that a self-evident proposition is not only self-evidently true, it is also self-evidently necessary. That is, your grasp of a self-evident truth teaches you not that it just happens to be true, but that it has to be true.

The intellectual faculty you are exercising when the necessary truth of a self-evident proposition dawns on you was referred to by Aristotle with the Greek word *nous*. We usually translate this as "intuition." This is the term used when Aristotle defines wisdom as "intuition and scientific knowledge of the most valuable things." To have scientific knowledge of a subject is to be in possession of demonstrations of the facts about it, and what intuition adds to that is insight into the necessary truth of the premises of those demonstrations. To have wisdom is to be in these two states with respect to the most valuable things. Very shortly we must say what "the most valuable things" are, but first, there's one more item to be covered under the heading of Aristotle's logic.

As I indicated above, you may have to do a lot of thinking, a lot of rearranging ideas and looking at them from different angles, before a principle that is evident in itself becomes evident to you. But this process isn't entirely haphazard. There is a method, or a set of strategies, to be used in this process. The fifth book of Aristotle's Organon summarizes these strategies. Its title is the *Topics*. "Topic" is the name given to any one of the strategies discussed. The logical gambits described in this book are useful not only for working your way up to understanding and seeing the truth of scientific principles, but also, as Aristotle says, for "intellectual training" and "ordinary conversations" (ordinary conversations of the argumentative sort, that is). The general name for the art which practices these methods is "dialectic."

In general, dialectic makes use of syllogisms and of inductive arguments. Inductive arguments infer general principles from specific instances, or draw conclusions about an entire class on the basis of a sample taken from it. Syllogisms you already know. Dialectical syllogisms differ from scientific syllogisms in that their premises, rather than being self-evident truths, are drawn from the opinions held by either everybody, most people, or the wise (experts), and in the latter case by either all of the wise, most of them, or the most respected among them. If you'll think about it, those are precisely the sources we do commonly appeal to in establishing the premises of most of our arguments.

The way it works out in practice is this: Aristotle typically begins a treatise on one of the sciences by reviewing the opinions of earlier philosophers, as well as popular thinking on the topic. He doesn't just summarize these opinions, he considers the evidence for and against each of them. In the process, he identifies the basic data the science must account for and the problems it must solve. He also isolates what may be taken as the "established results" of previous thinking. The second book or second chapter of a treatise typically takes a new tack and sets up a line of reasoning leading up to Aristotle's own first principle of the science. This is usually a definition—of nature, of the soul, of happiness, just to take three examples. There are places where Aristotle says that the first principles are always definitions, but some of his examples of first principles don't look much like definitions. One such is, "Equals subtracted from equals yield equals." After formulating a principle, Aristotle shows how it integrates previous results, accounts for the data of the science, and solves the problems previously identified. He does these things by constructing demonstrations which take his newly proposed first principle as one of their premises.

The general pattern of a scientific treatise is thus like going over a mountain:

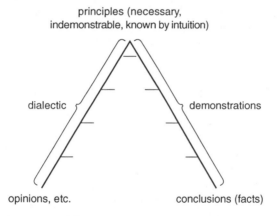

The facts that will form the conclusions of your demonstrations are either in your possession at the outset or are established in the course of the dialectical process. Also in this process, conflicting opinions or alternative hypotheses are weighed against each other to see how they stack up against the established facts and against criteria like consistency and simplicity. And various lines of reasoning and analogies are explored as possible sources or indicators of new hypotheses or potential first principles. The exact course of this process will naturally vary from one science to another.

For the sake of completeness, I should mention the final book of the *Organon*, called *On Sophistical Refutations*. This is a kind of supplement to the *Topics*, in which Aristotle tries to prepare the reader to deal with people who offer bad arguments—arguments that are either invalid (but give an appearance of validity) or that take as their premises what look like generally accepted opinions but aren't (because they are similar to or appear to follow from what really are generally accepted opinions). In a general over-view of Aristotle's philosophy, there is no need to look at this work in detail.

What Wisdom Knows

We've now covered two of the components of Aristotle's defini-tion of "wisdom": scientific knowledge and intuition. One more remains. For to be wise, says Aristotle, you must have scientific knowledge and intuition about "the most valuable things." To say what Aristotle thought these are is not difficult. To do justice to his treatment of them would be impossible in a brief survey like this. One of them we will only mention. The others we will spend a little more time on, because of their intrinsic interest, but we can only examine a small part of what Aristotle has to say about them.

The most valuable things fall into three classes: (1) the most universal principles and causes pertaining to those attributes which belong to things simply by virtue of the fact that they exist at all; in other words, the principles of "being qua being"; the sci-ence of these principles and attributes is called "metaphysics"; (2) the soul; and (3) the gods.

Aristotle's *Metaphysics* deals with concepts like being, sub-stance, unity, infinity, actuality and potentiality, and explicates and inventories the varieties of modes of opposition, part-whole relations, unity and plurality, universal and particular, and the kinds of substance, processes, and causes there are. Book Five is a kind of philosopher's dictionary of these and other terms, 30 of them in all, and some of them receive extensive treatment in other parts of the work. Besides clarifying terminology, the work exam-ines a number of basic principles, including the principle of noncontradiction, and attempts to answer various questions and solve various problems connected with these basic notions and principles. Since some of these matters have already been dealt with above, and others will come up in the discussions to follow, and not least because the *Metaphysics* is so complicated and diffi-cult, we will bypass all of this now and go on to discuss the soul.

The Soul

We are interested in two questions under this heading: What exactly *is* the soul? and Is the soul immortal?

To appreciate Aristotle's perspective on the soul, you must realize that the Greeks generally used that word to refer to whatever it is that is responsible for the life of an organism, whether they thought of it as breath, blood, something in the blood, "vital fire," or something else. Accordingly, every organism, including not only nonhuman animals but even plants, was thought to have a soul. There were, of course, important differences between human souls and those of other organisms, but they were all souls. Aristotle keeps to this way of thinking, and his search for a definition of the soul is consequently not a quest for what distinguishes the human from all other forms of existence, but an attempt to identify what distinguishes the living from the nonliving. This conception of soul continued to be the norm long after Aristotle's day, in fact right up to the time of Descartes in the sixteenth century. This means, incidentally, that the people who formulated the theological doctrines of the soul in the major Western religions—Christianity, Judaism, and Islam—were working in this tradition. (This tradition is reflected in our use of the terms "animate" and "inanimate"; *anima* is the Latin word for "soul.")

Given this approach, "soul" is basically a biological category. But to devise a definition of the soul, Aristotle resorted to the metaphysical concepts of actuality and potentiality.

In their simplest versions, "actuality" and "potentiality" meant the same thing for Aristotle that they mean in modern English—not surprising, since the English meanings derive from Aristotle's. But Aristotle added some more elaborate connotations to these terms. First, he associated potentiality with the idea of matter, and actuality with that of form. This seems straightforward enough, if you recall the statue we talked about in analyzing the four causes. At the beginning of the process of sculpting, the matter of the process—the block of marble—is potentially a statue. At the end, having received the form the sculptor has imposed on it, it is actually a statue. Aristotle's general definition of "change" is that it is "the actualization of what is potential."

Second, Aristotle emphasized something that we tend to forget (or take for granted without thinking about it), that in order to make something, you have to start with the right kind of matter. A block of marble is potentially several things, but it is not potentially everything. This is so because, in addition to being potentially several things, it is actually something, namely, a block of marble. Its potentiality is specific because of the actual characteristics it possesses. The notion of potentiality is thus not to be identified with possibility in a broad sense. It refers to the specific possibilities of a specific matter. Only prime matter is capable of becoming everything, and prime matter is not available as a raw material to anybody.

The third thing to remember about actuality and potentiality is that they can, as it were, be "stacked." You recall the point made earlier that the end of one process can become the matter for another: a geological process produces marble which the quarrying process turns into a block which the sculptor turns into a statue which the painter turns into a painted statue. Which things play the roles of matter, form, agent, and end depends on which process you're looking at. Since actuality and potentiality correspond to form and matter, the same is true of them. What is considered an actuality from one point of view, say, the characteristics of a block of marble, is potentiality from the point of view of the sculptures which that block might become. As you ascend through such a stack, the kind of potentiality and actuality you are looking at changes.

Fourth, Aristotle distinguished two senses of "potential." The one I've been talking about so far represents the capability of a matter to receive a form, which we might refer to as "passive potential," or "receptivity." The other sort of potentiality is the ability of a substance to *do* something, the power to act. This could be called "active potentiality" or "potency" or "power." (But in speaking of "power," you must not think of "energy" in some generic sense; in Aristotle, it refers to specific abilities.)

For a good example of the difference between the two kinds of potentiality, and more especially of how the two are related, consider the learning of a simple skill, like riding a bicycle. Say you're six years old and you're about to have your first riding lesson. You're a person of average strength and coordination (for a six-year old) and therefore perfectly capable of acquiring this skill. We might say, "You can ride a bike," meaning that although you haven't learned how yet, you are certainly a potential bike rider. You "have potential" as a bike rider. This is what I have called "receptivity"; you are in a position to receive the form which is the skill of bike riding. Now suppose we come to visit a couple of weeks later and ask how your training is coming. "I can do it now," you say. You have acquired the skill, you have achieved a certain level of mastery. You now have the power, the active potentiality, to ride a bike. This potentiality is the actualization of the passive potentiality you had two weeks earlier. But it is still a potentiality because you are sitting in the living room talking about it, rather than out demonstrating it. If I now ask you to do that, you actualize this potentiality by actually engaging in the activity itself. So we have a stack of three levels: passive potentiality, active potentiality, and activity.

Aristotle exploits these enrichments of the notions of actuality and potentiality in order to define the soul. As a good biologist, Aristotle defines life in terms of the activities or functions carried out by organisms, from things like respiration and nutrition to higher-order functions like sensation and thinking. To be alive is to have the power to carry out such activities. If the soul is what is responsible for an organism's being alive, then it must be the source of this active potentiality. But the source, or cause, of an active potentiality is just a certain form possessed by the substance which has this potentiality. The active potentiality of riding a bike is just the form constituted by the skill of riding a bike. Hence, the soul will be that form which enables an organism to carry out life-functions.

But what is that form? Aristotle could give only a partial answer to this question, because his knowledge of biology was pretty limited. But one advantage of Aristotle's approach to science was that he was able to give partial answers which left room for further developments. To appreciate his definition of the soul, we need to consider what the matter is which receives this form. The soul is an active potentiality which has been received by a matter which possessed the passive potentiality for receiving just such a form. What kind of matter is capable of receiving the power of life? Aristotle says that a "naturally organized body" is such a matter— that is, a body which has different organs for carrying out different functions is the kind of matter that can be alive. The soul is the form which renders such a being alive. The soul, in short, is the form of a living body.

But exactly what kind of form is this? There seem to be two possibilities. In the earlier discussion of nature and my ballpoint pen, I said that one thing "form" can refer to is the *design* of a thing, which can be identified with its nature when the design is responsible for the thing's having the power to behave in the way that it does. If this is the sense of "form" in effect in the definition of the soul, then the soul is identical with the pattern or structure whereby the different subsystems of the body are integrated into a unified whole. In that case, the structures of individual subsystems would be like parts of the soul. And to study anatomy and physiology would be to study the soul and its parts.

But another thing "form" can refer to is a state of activity. In my earlier example, if I am walking, then "walking" is a form of which I am the subject, or the matter. Similarly, if I am seeing a sunset or feeling the sun's warmth, my sense organs are in a certain state of activity. Aristotle often describes the soul in a way which has suggested to many interpreters that it is this kind of form. He says, for example, that if the eye had a soul, its soul would be sight. But here he is referring, not to the activity of actually seeing, but to the ability to see. The eye, as a physical organ, possesses the passive potentiality for sight. The power of sight, as a form imposed on the eye, is the active potentiality for seeing, and seeing is the activity in which that power comes to fruition. The question at issue here is whether that active potentiality or power is to be equated with the design of the matter (in this case, the organ), as I suggested in the previous paragraph, or is itself a state of activity on which the final state of activity (actually seeing) is somehow imposed.

If the latter alternative is confusing, let me suggest an example to clarify it. Think of an automobile sitting in the driveway. We can distinguish the matter of the car, the parts of which it is composed, from its form, the pattern or design into which these parts are organized and which would be illustrated in a blueprint or diagrammatic ("exploded") drawing of the car. Now suppose we get into the car and crank it up. Now we're sitting there with the engine running. We might describe the relationship between the car a minute ago and the car now by saying that a new form has been added to it. That new form is the state of activity which consists in the engine's running. And the matter on which that form has been imposed is the complex of design-plus-parts which we earlier identified as a form and a matter. Because the engine is running, the car is now capable of being driven out the driveway and down the street. Because the car is going (the engine is running), it is capable of going (travelling down the street). The former state of activity is the active potentiality for the latter state of activity.

Our question for Aristotle could then be stated: Is the soul as the form of the body like the design of the car (the disposition of its parts), or is it comparable to the running of the engine (a state of activity)? Is the power of sight to be identified with the structure of the eye or with a state of activity in it? In other words, is having a certain structure (in an appropriate matter) ipso facto to have the power of seeing, or is the power of seeing some other form to be added to what already has an appropriate structure? Is an appropriately organized body already alive, or must some condition of activity or activation be added to it to make it alive?

In modern times we tend to think of a state of activity as something that can be analyzed in terms of things in motion, and indeed this can be done for something like the running of an engine. But we must remember that there are other things that qualify as actualities and as active potentialities which cannot be so analyzed. Our notion of "potential energy" fits this description, and so does our idea of the charge on an electron or proton. Both of these refer to the power that a thing has to act in a certain way, and neither of them can be analyzed either as the design of the object or as a pattern of internal motion of the parts of the object. Perhaps Aristotle wants us to think of the soul as a state of activity in the same sense as the negative charge on an electron could be called a state of activity.

Unfortunately, Aristotle's views are simply not clear. Distinguishing the different things he might mean is helpful, I think, if we want to compare his views to those of later biologists, or if we want to imagine what an updated Aristotelianism would look like. But I don't think the distinctions I have been struggling with here make any difference for the next question we want to examine, which is, What are the implications of Aristotle's definition of the soul for the question of immortality? To make the following exposition simpler, I will proceed as if the previous issue had been settled in favor of the view that the soul is the overall structure of the body.

If immortality means the survival of the soul apart from the body, and if Aristotle's definition of the soul is correct, then immortality is impossible. The soul in principle could not exist apart from the body, any more than any other form can exist apart from the matter it informs. The shape of a statue can't exist all by itself, apart from the artist's medium. The qualities of coldness and dryness and the tendency to fall toward the center of the cosmos cannot exist apart from the earthy matter that possesses them. No more can the body's structure exist apart from the body that is structured. But Aristotle does not embrace this conclusion without qualification.

The human soul is complex. It has a part or aspect corresponding to the souls of plants (called the "vegetative" or "nutritive" soul); this part is responsible for the basic biological functions of the body. It has a part or aspect corresponding to the souls of non-human animals (called the "appetitive" soul); this part is responsible for our powers of sensation, desire, and movement. And it has a rational part or aspect, responsible for our reasoning abilities. Aristotle considers the possibility that some part of our soul escapes the definition he has given, that some part of the soul is not the form of a part of the body. The rational part is the only candidate for this position, since the vegetative and appetitive souls pretty obviously are necessarily bound up with bodily functions. If the rational part is not the form of a part of the body (is not embodied in any particular organ or organ system), then there is a possibility that it could survive the death of the body.

Aristotle says that we do have reason to suppose that the rational part of the soul is not the form of a part of the body. But he is willing to attribute immortality not to the entire rational part, but only to a part of this part. To understand this, we need to focus on what Aristotle considers the fundamental activity of the intellect, the formation of general concepts.

The general concept of a kind of thing is a form in the mind which corresponds to the form which defines that kind of thing out there in the world. Indeed, Aristotle says that your concept of a thing is the form of that thing in your mind. The form in the mind and the form in the object itself are the same, but they are embodied in different matters. This may be made clearer by an analogy. The form of a box, when embodied in cardboard, produces a box. If you draw a picture of a box, you're capturing the same form as a representation on paper. The form is the same, but the things are different because the matters are different. The same is true of things in the world compared to your concepts of them in your mind. The same can be said of sensation. Your visual image of a box is the form of a box as represented in your visual apparatus. It has the same shape as a box, or some analog to it, but it's made of flesh instead of cardboard. But intellection differs from sensation in two important ways. First, a concept is not a little copy of a particular object; it grasps what is common to all objects of a certain kind. A concept is what is articulated as a definition. A visual image of a box must be of a box having a certain shape and certain proportions, but a concept of a box is general—it applies to boxes of all shapes and sizes. Second, sensation is limited. Eyes can't hear, ears can't see. Further, eyes can see only a fraction of what might have been visible (if, for instance, we had been sensitive to infrared light and x-rays in addition to "visible light"). On top of that, what you can see depends on what you've been seeing: If you've been in bright light for a while, you're blind in sudden darkness, and vice versa. This kind of limitation is even more apparent in the case of touch: You can't tell whether something is warm or cool if it's at the same temperature as the hand you're feeling it with. All of these limitations derive, Aristotle says, from the matter (the organ) in which sensation is embodied. But the intellect suffers from no such limitations. There is nothing that you cannot think of. The mind is capable of taking on the form of anything whatsoever. In this respect, it is like prime matter. "It is necessary for it to be of no other nature," he says, "than that of potentiality."

Is the intellect a little piece of prime matter? If it is, it would seem to violate the principle that prime matter cannot exist by itself, without any form, which is just the idea that nothing can exist by itself without being some particular actual thing. But that's just the way the intellect seems to be before the forms of things have begun to be imposed on it. Another problem comes from the principle that a form can only be embodied in an appropriate matter. If you want to make a chair, you must start with the right kind of raw material. Some kinds of wood, metal, and plastic are serviceable; others are not. It would be hard to make a chair of rope or paper, and impossible to make one of water or oxygen. Each appropriate raw material will be composed of things which are ultimately composed of the elements which are so many different forms imposed on prime matter. So it would seem that forms and matters have to be stacked up in the right way, starting from prime matter, to produce the matter that will be capable of receiving the latest form, that of a chair. The intellect, however, seems to be able to receive the form which is the concept of a genus or species immediately, without having first received the intermediate forms that constitute the matter of the thing. Could prime matter do such a thing? Unfortunately, Aristotle never discusses these issues. The safest interpretation would seem to be to leave prime matter as the basis for what we call the "physical" world, and assume that the matter of intellect is a unique kind of thing that is just similar in some ways to prime matter.

At any rate, the fact that the intellect is capable of receiving the forms of all things is sufficient evidence for Aristotle to conclude that it could not be the form of part of the body because it would then be limited in somewhat the way that the sense organs are—whatever particular formal characteristics it possessed in itself would limit the forms it could perceive.

This is only a part of Aristotle's picture of the intellect, however. The part of the intellect we have been discussing is capable of receiving the forms of all things. But what is the agent that imposes these forms on this matter? You might suppose that the agent cause of our concept of a box is a box that we have seen, or perhaps our visual representation of a box. But this won't do, because of the differences between the particular box we see and the general concept we have in our minds. From the whole set of visual images of boxes, the intellect must abstract those common features which define them all as boxes. Aristotle says that just as vision requires not only the eye and the visible object, but also the action of light, so intellection requires not just experience of objects and the receptive intellect, but also some other active power. Hence, we must postulate a second part of the intellect, responsible for its power of conceptualization. This part Aristotle calls the "active intellect" or "agent intellect," as opposed to the "passive intellect" which receives and contains our concepts.

Neither part of the intellect (neither part of the rational part of the soul) is a form of a bodily organ. But Aristotle is willing to claim immortality only for the active intellect. His reasoning here is not entirely clear, but it seems to be something like this. What is to be immortal must be eternal, and to be eternal, it must be immune to change. In order to be immune to change, a thing must have no matter in its composition, for matter is the principle of potential for change. The agent intellect can be thought of as actuality or activity without any matter—a thing whose entire nature consists of the power to produce concepts—but the passive intellect is nothing but matter. Hence, only the agent intellect can be immortal.

This outlook offers us very little of what most people hope for from a proof of immortality. The part of the soul said to be immortal has no "contents"—no memories, no emotions, no desires, and no personal character. All that makes my soul mine is said to die with the body. The pure intellectual power which persists doesn't seem to retain anything of me about it. Perhaps that is why the concept of immortality isn't especially important in Aristotle's philosophy, with one possible exception. In his ethical theory, he recommends that we try to "partake of immortality" as far as possible. Whether such advice is consistent with his view of the soul, I leave you to judge after you have examined his ethical thought in more detail.

As I have repeatedly indicated, Aristotle's account of the rational soul is pretty sketchy. The attempt to fill in the gaps occupied Aristotelians for the next several centuries. A lot of attention focused on the agent intellect and in particular on the question as to how many agent intellects there had to be. Does each rational being have its own agent intellect, or is one agent intellect enough to do the job for everybody? The debate was complicated by the fact that Aristotle described the gods as existing in pure actuality, apart from all matter, and as essentially intellects. This led some of Aristotle's followers to identify the monotheistic God with the agent intellect, and thus to make God the author of all our concepts. The Arab commentators on Aristotle, in particular, spent a lot of time arguing about this.

The Gods

Aristotle's conception of the nature of a god is difficult, as I've just indicated. But his proof of the existence of a god is not so hard to follow. So I'll start here with the proof, and afterwards add a few remarks on what he thinks a god is like.

The proof runs roughly like this: We see that things are in motion all around us. Now some motions are caused by others. For in general, motion occurs when a potential agent comes into contact with a receptive matter. The motion which brings them together thus indirectly brings about the motion which the agent causes in the matter. It seems that all the motions in our cosmos can be traced back to the motions of the heavenly spheres, the spheres that carry the planets and the stars. Their revolutions are responsible for the seasons, which are responsible for all growth and life. And they keep the basic elements of earth, air, fire, and water stirred up so that they don't separate and thus bring all chemical processes to an end.

We can infer that motion is eternal, that is, that there never was a time when nothing was in motion. For if there were a time when nothing was in motion, then for motion to begin, a potential agent would have to be brought into contact with a receptive matter, and to do this would be to move something. Hence, motion could not begin unless it had already begun. But this is impossible. Therefore, since there is motion now, it is impossible that there ever was a time when there was no motion.

It seems that not only is motion eternal, but there are some particular motions that go on continuously and eternally, namely the motions of the heavenly spheres. If motion is eternal, and these motions are responsible for all others, then these motions must be eternal.

Whatever is in motion is moved by some cause. If the moving cause is itself in motion, then it must be moved by some other cause. And similarly for that cause. But this series cannot go on to infinity. No actual thing or series of things can be infinite, for existence requires determinateness and limits—whatever exists must be finite. Accordingly, motion must always be traceable to some cause which is not in motion: an unmoved mover.

The nature of every natural object is an unmoved mover. It causes motion without itself being in motion, except incidentally. But most natures are responsible for temporary motions in perishable substances, and may therefore be regarded as themselves perishable. An eternal motion, however, must have an eternal unmoved mover as its cause. Therefore, there exists some eternal unmoved cause of motion. In fact, for each eternal motion there must be a different unmoved cause. Whatever the number of the heavenly spheres (a point over which astronomers differ), there are also that many eternal unmoved movers.

Each eternal unmoved mover is a god. While an unmoved mover is not, by definition, in motion, it is in a state of activity or actuality. In fact, Aristotle says that being in a state of actuality is of the very essence of an unmoved mover. There are some activities that do not involve motion or any other process. Thought can be this kind of activity. And thought seems the noblest of activities. So this must be the activity of the gods. Apparently what Aristotle means by "thought" here is not consciousness of a sequence of ideas. That kind of thought is "moving" from one idea to another. The thought of an eternal unmoved mover is rather the unchanging awareness of a single object. And that object is the god itself. The eternal, unchanging activity of a god is self-awareness. At one point Aristotle says that a god's thinking is the thinking of thinking.

I said earlier that the nature of any natural thing can be described as an unmoved mover. But this is only relatively speaking. Your nature in a sense moves around with you as you move. It would be strange to say that your nature is in the same place as you or that it walks around. But it would be even stranger to say that it is somewhere else or stays put while you're walking. Your nature is just an aspect of you, and as such, it shares in whatever happens to you.

But the unmoved movers are unmoved in an absolute sense. There is no way in which they are in motion, either essentially or accidentally. How then do they create motion in the heavenly spheres? Aristotle says that they evoke motion in the way that the object of desire does. When you perceive or even imagine something you desire, you are prompted to go after it, but this motion in you does not presuppose any motion on the part of what you desire. Just so, the heavenly spheres are moved as it were by their desire to emulate the eternal perfect activity of the unmoved movers. But having some matter, the closest they can come to such unmoving activity is to move eternally in perfect circles. It is the desire to be godlike which moves the heavenly spheres, which in turn causes all motion and change within the cosmos. This desire to imitate the god is a form of love, so for Aristotle it is quite literally true that love makes the world go around.

There is much that is obscure in Aristotle's conception of the gods, but this much is clear: He did not think of the gods as personal beings who intervene in any way in the course of human events. Prayer and sacrifice to these perfect intellects would be absurd, and the only kind of "communion" we can enjoy with them is imitation or participation, to the limit of our ability, in their kind of activity, by devoting ourselves as completely as possible to the life of the mind.

The investigation of the highest objects thus brings us by a roundabout path to the topic of how we ought to live our lives, and thus to the science of ethics. We will now bring that topic into the center of our attention, but we will approach it from a very different direction.

II

Aristotle's Ethics

Ethics, for Aristotle, is a science. It is what he calls a practical, rather than a theoretical, science. A theoretical science consists of knowledge pursued purely for the sake of knowing it. A practical science, on the other hand, is knowledge pursued "for the sake of action." That is, it is knowledge whose function is to guide our actions. In his treatise, *Nicomachean Ethics* (not his only ethical writing, but the only one we'll look at here), the topics Aristotle discusses, the order in which he takes them up, and the way he analyzes them are dictated by this conception of ethics as a science intended to guide the actions of human beings. The treatment is accordingly determined by Aristotle's own conceptions of science and of human actions and their motives. Eventually, we want to see how these presuppositions define his approach. But his ideas may be more accessible to us if we begin from a different angle.

It seems to me that from our standpoint, the key to Aristotle's ethics is his idea of *virtue*. We will eventually want to know what exactly a virtue is, how it fits into the overall scheme of Aristotle's ethics, and why he makes it the focal point of ethics. Answering these questions will finally lead us back to Aristotle's own way of approaching this science. But to begin with, I want to suggest an image that I think will help you appreciate Aristotle's point of view.

Think about a movie you've seen in which there were clearly identifiable heroes and villains. Cop movies, like *Lethal Weapon* or *Beverly Hills Cop*, are good examples, but there are many others, too. Now I want you to reflect on how you recognized the villains as villains. The tip-off that somebody is a bad guy is that he (or sometimes, she) does something bad—something unjust and preferably contemptible. The extent of his villainy is revealed either by the awfulness of his crimes or by the number of them, and usually both. To make things perfectly clear, the director or screenwriter will often have the villain do something outrageous right near the beginning, like the crime boss who drowns the guy in concrete in *Lethal Weapon III*. Thereafter, a whole series of misdeeds confirms and deepens our judgment that the boss is no good, and works up our antipathy to the point that we feel the villain deserves what the hero does to him in the end—or worse. Movies such as this are seldom subtle, and the villain's misdeeds are never ambiguous. We know, because our parents and teachers keep telling us, that the better sort of films, the ones we ought to watch more of, are subtle and full of ambiguities, complex rather than simplistic, and thus more realistic. But then, one of the reasons we like these movies is because they're so much easier to deal with than real life. Everything is so much clearer in escape films. And that's also the advantage they offer us in the present context.

Think about your reaction to a villainous deed of the villain. The act is clearly wrong. You don't have to stop and think about its moral status, mull it over and weigh the possible arguments that could be offered in defense of it, or consider the mitigating circumstances. Your reaction—outrage, indignation, enmity toward the perpetrator, at least condemnation—is spontaneous and powerful. This reaction is simultaneously emotional and intellectual, for in feeling the emotions you feel you have at the same time passed judgment on the act that provoked them and the character who performed that act. If you express that judgment, you might not use the language I have used, calling the act unjust or immoral. That kind of language is unpopular nowadays. You would probably just label the villain with a term of reproach corresponding to the strength of your feeling—creep, jerk, bastard, asshole.

The instinctive reaction you have had is one which you would say is appropriate to the action that provoked it. It's appropriate in the sense that anybody ought to react that same way. If people didn't react that way, we would say there was something wrong with them. They're at least weird. And if they consistently fail to react appropriately to hateful acts, we begin to suspect that they are little better than the perpetrators of such acts. To be a regular, decent sort of person, it's not enough that you don't *do* bad things; you also have to have the appropriate emotional reaction to them. And after all, it's not as if feelings and actions were divorced. If you aren't emotionally repulsed by certain kinds of acts, what's to stop you from doing them yourself? Who would want to associate with a person whose only inhibition against assault or theft was the fear of punishment? We condemn the movie villain not just for what he or she does, but perhaps even more because he or she lacks the reactions which would keep him or her from doing it. And one of the reasons we identify with the hero—indeed, the main way we recognize him or her as the hero—is that through his or her actions, he or she demonstrates the same kind of emotional reactions to villainy that we feel.

These movies manipulate our emotions by presenting us with clear and simple situations and motivations, and because of this clarity and simplicity, we feel free to react instinctively to what we see. Other movies, and sometimes even parts of these same movies, are less simplistic. I would like to distinguish three levels of complexity, with the first being the least complex, the one we've been discussing so far. At the second level, we are presented with a situation in which we aren't sure what the appropriate feelings are, or consequently what the appropriate action is. The hero then takes action, and we see intuitively that this course of action was right. The hero's action thus resolves the ambiguity of the situation for us. This situation is unlike the ones previously described because our reaction is not automatic; that is, we don't know right away what to praise and what to blame. It only becomes obvious to us when we see what the hero has done. This situation resembles the previous ones in that our reaction is not a result of deliberation. It is less instinctive than in the earlier cases, but still to some extent spontaneous.

At the next level of complexity, our spontaneous reactions fail us entirely. We don't know how to feel about the action or situation we are confronted with, and no decisive heroic action will resolve the issue for us. Even after the protagonist has made his or her choice, there's room for doubt whether that choice was the right one. Our instincts give us no confident answer; we're just going to have to think about it.

Something that is important to remember about these three levels we've distinguished is that the first one serves as the basis for the other two. This is perhaps more obvious at the second level. I think the experience we have there could be described like this: The situation we confront asks us for a finer discrimination than we have exercised before. Our instinctive reactions seem to represent a rough-and-ready, get- the-general-idea perception of justice or of right and wrong. The new situation calls on us to sharpen this perception, to bring our instinctive reactions into better focus, to extract from them the principle that is somehow there and will resolve our dilemma, if only we can isolate it. The action taken by the hero then accomplishes this isolation for us. If we did not automatically react to clear situations the way we do—in the appropriate way—the rightness of the hero's solution would not be apparent to us.

How the third level of complexity relates to the first may be less clear. Here we are not trying to sharpen our perceptions but to put our principles into words and somehow integrate them with the facts of the case. It all seems very cerebral, especially because we do not assume—and here's where we could learn something from Aristotle—that our instinctive emotional reactions can be the sources of ethical principles. But consider this: When we're debating ethical questions, one of the main tactics we use for testing someone's assertions is to see how they stack up against what we regard as a clear case. For instance, when we're debating pacifism, one question that always comes up is, "What would you do if you were walking down a dark street and somebody attacked you?" The expected answer is "I would defend myself, with force if necessary," with the implication that this course of action would be justified. The antipacifist regards this answer as obviously correct. Why? Because we *instinctively* feel that it is justified. The tactic relies on an instinctive emotional reaction as a test of an articulated principle. Whether this tactic is successful in this particular case is another question. My point at present is simply that this is among the most common of argumentative strategies, and it illustrates how our instinctive reactions serve as the background or the basis for our articulated ethical beliefs. Again and again, we try to get clear about what is right or wrong by asking ourselves, about a host of different situations, "What would I do if . . . ?" And we answer these questions by envisioning how we would *feel* if. . . .

One reason for making these points is for the light they shed on people who say they are skeptical or just unsure of themselves with regard to ethical commitments. To be affected by the most accessible and most popular sort of story in the way intended by its creators, you must respond to the characters and events with feelings of which an ethical judgment is an inseparable part. Un-

less you do this, there is a real sense in which you don't understand what is going on. Of course, you can have the appropriate
feelings inside the movie house and then abandon them when you
walk out the door. But it's not clear why life should affect you so
differently from the way art does.

With the image of these instinctive reactions firmly in mind, we
can begin to move back toward Aristotle by realizing that, though
we have called them "instinctive," these reactions are largely
learned. Much of our upbringing consists of being trained to regard certain kinds of conduct and certain kinds of outcomes with
certain feelings. Teaching us what is right and wrong is, after all,
not primarily a matter of haranguing us with little moral sermons.
That may be a part of it, and may in particular be one *means* of
bringing about the desired result. But the intended effect is much
more to habituate us to be repulsed and angered by wrong, to
admire and emulate the right. (People of very different beliefs
nonetheless share a common bond if they instinctively love and
hate the same actions.) In feelings, as in actions, it is difficult to
distinguish precisely what derives from heredity from what derives from environment, and this is especially difficult when we
are considering *habitual* actions and feelings. It's no accident that
habit is sometimes referred to as "second nature." But it is clear at
any rate that the contribution of upbringing is substantial.

In talking about movies, I've focused on our reactions to the
behavior of others, but as I've already intimated, the same emotions that underlie our judgment of others also motivate our own
conduct. And our upbringing, in which our emotions are trained,
focuses on both of these. The people who raise us guide our reactions by telling us stories in film and other media, and by reward-
ing and punishing, praising and blaming our own actions. Nor to
be omitted is the impact on us of the example of people we spontaneously model our conduct on.

The result of all this is an acquired tendency to experience certain feelings when confronted with certain situations, feelings
which to a large extent determine both how we shall judge the
conduct of others in those situations and what course of action we
ourselves shall choose in those situations. Such a tendency is precisely the kind of thing a virtue is. Or, to use Aristotelian language,
this is the genus of virtue.

A genus, of course, is only half of a definition. We still need to know the specific difference. This is especially important in the present case, because the genus of virtue is also the genus of vice. The specific difference we're looking for is what distinguishes virtue from vice.

Our actions are determined by our emotions, and variations in action are due, therefore, to variations in emotion. The significant variations in our emotional reactions to situations are (a) what emotions are felt, and (b) how strongly felt the emotions are. The kind of emotions we feel can be either appropriate or inappropriate to the situation that evokes them. What I mean by "appropriate" emotions are those we would regard as normal under the circumstances or as relevant to those circumstances. For example, if one feature of a situation we find ourselves in is that it poses some threat to our welfare, then fear (or anxiety) is an appropriate emotion in the intended sense of "appropriate." To say this is to leave open the questions of how afraid or anxious we ought to be, how far this fear should be balanced by confidence, and what finally we ought to do. If the most conspicuous feature of a situation is that it is dangerous, then emotions like anger, embarrassment, or the inclination to eat something are inappropriate—they are simply out of place. These feelings and desires are appropriate to other situations. Of course, situations can be complex, they can possess features each of which renders a different emotion appropriate. If a thief invades a dinner party, holds you at gunpoint, and after relieving you of your valuables, insults you and then forces you to undress (to discourage you from pursuing him into the street), it would be appropriate to be afraid, angry, and embarrassed, and the inclination to engage in a gourmet repast may still be hovering in the background, if it hasn't been squeezed out by everything else. (But how could you be hungry at a time like that?) As you can tell, this business of feeling an appropriate emotion is less a matter of ethics than one of psychology. To feel an emotion not appropriate to the situation is to be mentally unbalanced.

Ethical considerations enter with the second variable in our emotions—how strongly the emotions are felt. Assuming that you're experiencing an emotion of an appropriate kind, given the kind of situation you're in, are you experiencing the appropriate strength or intensity of this emotion? How much of the emotion is appropriate?

The answer to this question, too, depends on the situation.

What you ought to feel (and what you ought to do) depends in fact on the very particular, concrete circumstances of the particular, concrete situation you happen to find yourself in at a given time. Aristotle repeatedly emphasizes the fact that there are so many possible variations in these particular circumstances and such a variety of possible actions, that it is not possible to formulate a criterion (or set of criteria) that will always tell you what to do. You can make a rule that is general enough that it is always right—such as "Do what is just," or "Be brave"—but then it's so general that it doesn't give much guidance. You can get more specific than this, but in doing so you have to recognize that the more specific the rule, the more exceptions it may admit. The more specific it is, the less it should be regarded as an absolute commandment and the more it should be treated as a guideline or rule of thumb.

We could make the same point, not in terms of rules or criteria, but in terms of habits. The more typical the situation you find yourself in, the safer it is to go through it on automatic pilot, just letting your habits control your actions. The less typical the situation, the more you need to wake up and make a judgment call on the right way to feel and act. But there is no method for deciding what to do which guarantees correct action on every occasion.

The definition of virtue we're about to give is so general that it gives no specific guidance on how to behave, but it does set up a framework within which to pursue answers to that question. We've got as far as asking, How strongly should we feel the emotion relevant to our situation? It's not very helpful to say, "the right amount." It only goes a little further if we observe that "the right amount" will be that which is neither too little nor too much—it is, in this sense, the moderate or mean amount. Uninformative as this might seem, it is enough to distinguish, in a general way, virtue from vice. The specific difference which defines virtue is that it represents the "moderate" amount of the relevant emotion. Habitually feeling either too little or too much of the emotion is a vice. This might be clearer if we consider some examples.

Anger is an appropriate response to a perceived injustice. But how angry should an injustice make you? This depends on a number of factors. Is it a clear and flagrant violation of someone's rights, or an ambiguous and perhaps unintended affront to someone's self-image? Is the victim being deprived of something significant or of something trivial? Is it a rare occurrence or part of a pattern of mistreatment? What is the relationship between victim and perpetrator? Are you the victim or are you reacting to someone else's victimization? It might be appropriate to forgive, and hence not get angry at, a rare and minor act of thoughtlessness on the part of a parent, child, or spouse, but appropriate to get angry at the same kind of act between strangers, and even more appropriate as the injury increases or is repeated.

A person who habitually feels the right amount of anger, as dictated by those sorts of circumstances, will be said to possess the virtue of being "even-tempered." A person who consistently tends to become more angry than the situation calls for is guilty of the vice of being "short-tempered" or (to use an older word) "irascible." (We could say "irritable" or "grouchy," but we tend to use these for temporary conditions, whereas a vice is more long-term.) On the other hand, a person who is consistently less angry than the situation calls for, who is harder to rile than he or she ought to be, suffers equally from a vice, though I'm not sure what the best name for it is. A concoction like "inirascibility" might do, or "imperturbability," though something with fewer syllables would be handy. Words like "meek," "doormat," "pushover," and "wimp" come to mind, but these all seem to connote a deficiency of self-confidence or perhaps an excess of timidity. But the inirascible person isn't afraid to react to an injustice, it just doesn't bother him or her the way it should.

For another example, we might consider courage. This virtue is unusual in that it involves not one emotion but two. Aristotle thinks of courage as striking the right balance between fear and self-confidence (or boldness). These emotions are appropriate to dangerous situations, and especially, Aristotle says, to the situation of being in battle. One who habitually feels an excess of fear and a deficient amount of confidence is a coward. A person who habitually feels too much boldness and not enough fear is foolhardy (rash, overconfident). Precisely how much of each emotion it is appropriate to feel depends, as always, on precisely what the circumstances are. While in some circumstances, courage would be evinced by standing one's ground, there are other situations in which retreating would be evidence of one's courage. This is one respect in which Aristotle's notion of courage differs from our own. I think we have also lost his recognition of excess boldness as a vice. Perhaps we don't recommend foolhardiness, but we do tend to admire it.

These examples perhaps give you a sense of what it means to say that a virtue corresponds to a "moderate" amount of an emotion. This is the specific difference distinguishing virtue from vice. If we put this together with the genus identified earlier, we can formulate a precise definition of virtue: *A virtue is an acquired tendency to experience certain feelings when confronted with certain situations (feelings which largely determine how we judge the conduct of others and what course of action we ourselves shall choose) and to experience these feelings in a moderate degree (neither too strongly nor too weakly) as called for by the specific circumstances of the situation.*

There are some points already mentioned or implied by our examples that need to be explicitly stated and emphasized to avoid misunderstanding this definition. When Aristotle or Aristotelians say that virtue consists in a "mean," we must not be misled into thinking that there is some particular measure of emotion that is the right one in every relevant situation—into thinking, for example, that some particular mix of boldness and fear will always constitute courage in every dangerous situation. The appropriate amount of emotion, and hence the location of the "mean" on the spectrum of strength of emotion, varies with the situation. The mean is usually described as being "between two extremes," but that language is misleading. The "extremes" here are not like the ends of a line segment, with the mean being represented by the precise midpoint of the segment. The mark representing the mean can fall at any point on the line, and the "extremes," the vices, are any amount either more or less than the right amount. Anything other than the right amount is a wrong amount. One consequence of thinking this way about the mean is that the mean can sometimes be rather extreme; that is, in some circumstances the appropriate amount of an emotion to feel may be the maximum amount. Some situations, for example, may call for you to get as angry as you can get.

Similar remarks apply to the description of "moderation" as the defining characteristic of virtue. When we speak of something as "moderate," we think of it as being in the middle of the range of possibilities. This is not Aristotle's meaning. Doubtless he *would* say that the majority of situations we encounter call for a reaction somewhere in the middle of the range of possibilities. Situations calling for extreme anger are relatively rare. If we made a graph plotting the intensity of emotion called for against the number of situations calling for a given intensity, it would probably form a bell curve. In that sense, Aristotle's ethics could be said to be an ethics of moderation. But it is consistent with this to insist that sometimes the right thing to do is to become extremely irate (or bold, or proud, or whatever).

The definition of virtue is sufficient to distinguish virtue from vice. But, of course, we want more specific information. We would really like to have a method for determining precisely the right thing to do in every situation. But as I pointed out earlier, Aristotle thinks that such a thing can't be had. The factors that determine the right thing to feel and do admit of too many variations. It is possible, however, to give some general guidelines. One way to do that is to define and characterize each of the virtues by identifying the emotion or emotions of which it is the "mean," naming the two vices opposed to each virtue, and describing the typical kinds of behavior that exemplify each virtue and its opposed vices in typical kinds of situations. This is the sort of thing I've done very sketchily in the examples I've given, but of course it could be carried out in much more detail and for all of the virtues. I won't attempt that here. If you want to see Aristotle's list of the virtues and vices, see the appendix to this chapter. His own discussions of each virtue occur in Book III Chapter 6 through Book V (1115a3–1138b15) of the *Nicomachean Ethics*.

Another way of providing ethical guidelines would be to formulate *rules* telling you what to do—a set of commandments or catalog of dos and don'ts. We could extract some rules of conduct from Aristotle's discussions of the individual virtues, especially since he gives examples there of virtuous and vicious behavior. But he doesn't take that approach himself. A concern with rules seems more appropriate to what might be called a "legalistic" ethics, which emphasizes keeping a tally of your good and bad deeds, understood as acts of obedience to and violation of such rules. Such an ethics focuses on your actions, on your "track record," rather than on your character, and tempts us to equate character with your score or batting average of good and bad deeds. When it considers virtue at all, a legalistic ethics tends to reduce all virtues to the virtue of obedience and all vices to the vice of disrespect, with both of these being directed in the first place toward the rules themselves, and ultimately (for some moralists) toward the author(s) of these rules (usually God). Such an ethics fits well into a scheme which promises rewards and punishments corresponding exactly to our good and bad actions. Aristotle's ethics, in contrast, is concerned with the kind of person you are, rather than with every single act you perform. It does not assume that every one of your actions must somehow be taken into account in determining what you are. You may sometimes do something that is literally out of character, and punishment or restitution may be called for, but it doesn't necessarily go on your record till the end of time. Good people may sometimes do bad things without ceasing to be good people. That doesn't make a wrong act any less wrong, but it does make it less "final."

But I think the main reason Aristotle avoids giving us rules of conduct is that rules look too absolute, too exceptionless. Giving out rules encourages people to overlook the sometimes subtle variations in circumstances that make the difference between good and bad action. Following a rule sometimes results in doing the wrong thing.

You may protest that we need some guidance more specific than Aristotle gives us. I think he would agree, but he would say that what you want is already ready to hand in your own culture. The same social group that inculcated certain habits in you also taught you certain rules. Aristotle assumes that you come to the study of ethics with those as part of your baggage. Some of those rules are absolute prohibitions: Thou shalt not murder. But most of them take the form of proverbs or sayings that express the conventional wisdom about how to behave. These have the advantage that they don't look quite so much like absolutes. In fact, a curious thing about such proverbial wisdom is that there are often pieces of it in the same culture that seem to point in different directions. A penny saved is a penny earned, but nothing ventured, nothing gained. A stitch in time saves nine, the early bird gets the worm, opportunity knocks but once, and better three hours too soon than a minute too late, but look before you leap because haste makes waste, and never accept the first offer. The same culture that taught you these proverbs hopefully also gave you a sense of when to appeal to them for guidance; that is, they taught in what sorts of situation thrift, caution, promptness, and so on should be emphasized, and in what sorts we should encourage ourselves to be liberal, take risks, and go slowly. This situation fits neatly into Aristotle's notion that virtue consists in a mean. The most common use of proverbs is to nudge you back in one direction or the other when someone thinks your behavior is straying too far from the middle course.

One difference between Aristotle's ethics and the ethics we have inherited from our immediate ancestors is that our own ethics tends more toward the legalistic viewpoint. A second difference can be located in our traditional conception of what virtue itself is. We seldom think about virtue in general, but we do sometimes think of certain people or actions as brave, or temperate, or generous, or unselfish. We may not use those exact words, but our conception of the person or action corresponds to the way these words have been used in our recent history. If asked to explain what one of these virtues is, we would probably try to describe a situation in which the virtue is clearly exemplified. We would almost certainly pick a situation in which a person is strongly tempted to do the wrong thing, and then define the virtue as "what it takes" to do the right thing despite the temptation. We tend to define virtue as the ability to overcome temptation, which means the ability to overcome those desires of ours which urge us either to do the wrong thing or not to do the right thing. We seldom give much thought to what kind of thing this ability might be. To the extent that we ignore the psychology behind right conduct (or wrong conduct), the names of the virtues tend to degenerate into mere labels, awarded like blue ribbons for certain kinds of behavior. If we're not content to think of a virtue as something mysterious that you've either got or you haven't got (like "charisma" or "cool"), we think of it as consisting in an act of sheer willpower by which one overcomes the wrong desire. But willpower is also a pretty mysterious phenomenon. We end up with very little notion of how to inculcate virtue or motivate right behavior, in ourselves or in others.

I think Aristotle would agree with our notion of virtue in one respect: He would agree that a situation in which we confront powerful desires to do things that are not virtuous is the best test of virtue. It is in such a situation that you get clear evidence as to how strong a person's virtue is. But he would reject the idea that "the ability to overcome strong desires" is a good definition of virtue. For in Aristotle's view, virtue is what might be called a modification of desire. It is a tendency, as we have said, to feel the appropriate intensity of an appropriate desire in reaction to the situation you are in. The true mark of a virtuous person is that in most situations, he or she does not even desire to do what is wrong in the first place. If you want to understand what virtue is, you should not think of the restraint it might require to refrain from doing violence to your worst enemy when he or she is being particularly provoking; you should think rather of your instinctive reaction to the movie villain who kills in cold blood. You have been brought up to feel automatic disapproval of murder, and that same feeling keeps you from even considering the possibility, under normal circumstances, of killing someone. Moreover, under abnormal circumstances, when your anger has been aroused so that you actually want to kill someone, your habitual feelings constitute one of the primary sources of your ability to overcome that desire. A person who has been trained to regard murder with horror is much less likely to murder in a fit of rage than a person who has not. And it will take a much more powerful surge of violent rage to bring the well-trained person to kill than to do the same thing to a person who lacks such training. Mark Twain tells about a prospector in a mining camp in the old West who wrote in his diary, "Had to shoot my partner today. He started putting on airs." To a person who lacks the proper upbringing, vicious conduct comes easily. Temptation involves no great struggle, for there is little or nothing there to oppose the wrong desire. On the other hand, the more solidly engrained your virtue is, the easier it will be for you to moderate your desires, to bring them back within the bounds of appropriateness when circumstances are especially provoking. That's why situations of temptation represent a good test of your virtue. We could say that it is a property of virtue that one who possesses it can better withstand temptation. And the definition of virtue enables one to understand why it possesses that property.

From what we have said, you should be able to see some of the advantages (and perhaps also some of the disadvantages) of making virtue the key notion of ethics. But there is one very important advantage, from Aristotle's point of view, that we have not mentioned yet. Aristotle is trying to construct ethics *as a science*. Ideally, a science demonstrates that certain facts are necessary. One kind of necessity—logical or mathematical—just depends on the principles and rules of our logical and mathematical systems. But the scientist is interested in necessary facts out there in the world beyond our systems. And out there, necessity depends on the natures of things. Things must behave the way they do because they are the kinds of things they are. The science of psychology, for example, studies human nature. It tells us about the kinds of things that human beings do. But in so doing, it merely spells out a range of possible behaviors, within which both virtues and vices must fall. Ethics is concerned with a selection from among those possible behaviors; it is concerned with how we are habituated to choose some possibilities (the virtuous acts) rather than others (the vicious). Since virtues and vices are learned, they are not natural, in the strictest sense of the term. But they can still become the subject of a science, because they are habits, and habits are similar to natures. They are, as the saying goes, "second nature." Habits are not as invariant in their operation as (first) natures, and consequently ethics cannot fulfill the scientific ideal as perfectly as mathematics or physics. But in the domain of action, they're the closest things to natures that we can get. This is how Aristotle's conception of science renders virtue the natural point of focus for ethical studies.

Aristotle does not, however, begin the *Nicomachean Ethics* with a discussion of virtue. He starts much further back, with his conception of ethics as the science intended to guide the actions of human beings. Action is a kind of change, and from our study of the four causes we know that the character of a change is always determined by its end. Aristotle begins, accordingly, with an investigation of the ends of human actions. In the case of human action, the end can also be described as a purpose or goal; it is that for the sake of which the action is done. The end of our action is in each case something which is good, or which appears to us to be good, in one or another sense of "good." In order to serve as a guide to action, ethics must give us a general conception of the ends or goods that can be achieved through action.

Some ends are subordinate to others; that is, the ends of some actions or activities become materials or tools for other activities with further ends. To use Aristotle's own example, the end of the art of bridle-making is a bridle, but the bridle is a tool to be used in the art of riding. And the art of riding is adapted to the use of horses in other activities. Aristotle mentions particularly their use in war-making. The art of riding is thus subservient to the art of generalship (strategy and tactics). But war is itself an instrument of public policy, so that the art of generalship is subordinate to the art of government (which Aristotle calls "politics").

The observation that some ends (and their corresponding activities) are subordinate to other ends (and *their* corresponding activities) leads Aristotle to ask whether there is some one end that somehow subsumes under itself or integrates into itself *all* the ends we pursue and hence all the activities we engage in. He notes that we generally assume that there is such an end and we are pretty much agreed on its name—we call it "happiness." But there's a lot of disagreement and not a lot of clarity about what the thing is that "happiness" names. So the first task of ethics is to figure out what happiness is.

What we are after is the end appropriate to a human being qua human being. Ends shared with other sorts of beings are therefore out of the question, and so also are ends specific only to some human beings, such as the ends of particular arts and crafts. Ends shared with nonhuman beings, such as getting enough to eat, may be necessary conditions for being happy, but they aren't what human happiness is all about. And more particular ends, like being a good guitarist, may be ingredients in *my* happiness, conceived as something peculiar to me, but they aren't part of a general conception of human happiness.

Now the end or good of an action can be either something separate from the action itself, as the product is separate from the act of manufacturing it, or it can be something not separable from the action. The end of a musical performance, for example, is not something over and above the performance itself. The music *is* the performance of the music. In looking for the end that governs all our actions, we are looking for the end or purpose of a human life. For your life, in one important sense of the term, is just the sum total of your actions. The end which is the goal of human life must surely not be some product apart from that life itself. What distinguishes the life which is lived well from the life lived poorly must be some feature of the life which is lived well. (This may not be as obvious to you as it seems to have been to Aristotle.)

Aristotle notes that in the case of something like fluit-playing, the good consists in doing well those things which flutists qua flutists do. That is, if you specify the function that defines a flutist, then the mark of a good flutist is to perform that function well.

This seems to apply to actions generally. So Aristotle asks whether there is some function that belongs to the human being qua human being. The answer is that there is. The human being is the rational animal, the animal whose property it is to reason. We might therefore define the human good as "reasoning well."

But what does reasoning well mean? Part of what reasoning means is trying to understand and explain things, to investigate things scientifically and to figure out exactly what you want and the best way to get it. Doing these things well means exercising the skills we associate with "critical thinking": formulating questions and problems carefully, considering relevant evidence and alternatives, arguing logically, making appropriate distinctions, evaluating arguments and options in accord with established canons, and so on. If you do these things, then you will possess what Aristotle called the "intellectual" virtues: good judgment, good deliberation, prudence, science, art (know-how), and intuition.

This is probably the sort of thing we would automatically think of as "reasoning well." But for Aristotle, this is only half of it. For "reasoning" refers to the activity of the rational part of the soul. And while the part which carries out the kinds of activities just mentioned is the rational part of the soul in the strict sense, there is also a second part which is, or can be, rational in an extended sense. This is the appetitive part of the soul, the part we share with other animals. This part does not reason, but it is capable of "listening to reason," of obeying the truly rational part as a child obeys a parent, or as a dog obeys its master. The appetitive part is the locus of the emotions, the passions which we can feel too strongly or too weakly relative to the situation which provokes them. To feel these emotions appropriately is to feel them in that measure which the rational part dictates (when the rational part is reasoning well). Hence, the appetitive part can be said to be "reasoning well" (in an almost metaphorical sense) when it acts in accord with the virtues as we have defined them above.

Aristotle uses the word "virtue" for both the intellectual excellences and the emotional ones we discussed earlier. He calls the former "intellectual virtues" and the latter "ethical virtues" (from *ethos*, "character"). The definition of virtue I gave earlier applies only to the ethical virtues.

The line of reasoning I have sketched leads Aristotle to define happiness as "activity of soul in accord with virtue." The life lived virtuously, the life characterized by the exercise of both critical thinking and appropriately moderated passion, is the happy life. Aristotle recognizes that to be truly happy, one must also be equipped with a modicum of material goods, for to lack the necessities of life would surely detract from happiness, and besides, some of the ethical virtues (generosity, for example) require the possession of material goods. He also stipulates that one's life must be decently long to qualify as happy, for "one swallow," he says, "does not make a spring." But these are what we might call peripheral ingredients of a happy life. The central requirement is activity in accord with virtue.

Having arrived at this definition, Aristotle then goes on to explicate ethical virtue along the lines we followed above, and later discusses the intellectual virtues and other topics related to ethics. We will not follow him here through the entirety of his ethics. But before we part company with him, there is one claim of his that we must take note of.

After his extended discussions of the happy life, Aristotle asks what mode of life is the *most* happy. For within the scope of the definition of happiness there is still room for a difference of emphasis. Some people pursue a more active, more involved lifestyle. For Aristotle, these terms don't mean getting lots of physical exercise; they mean taking part in the activities of social and political life: government, war, business, and so on. These are the spheres in which the ethical virtues in particular have a chance to shine. Other people pursue the "theoretical life": They engage primarily in scientific research and reflection. Obviously, this is the field of action primarily for the intellectual virtues. The crowning achievement of the active life is the virtuous exercise of the art of government. The crowning achievement of the theoretical life is the attainment of wisdom. Which way of life is better?

The rational part of the soul (in the strict sense of "rational") is the best part, says Aristotle, and it is the part which is most truly yourself. It is also the part which is most similar to a god. This is because the activity of reasoning is the human activity most like a god's activity, and the activity of intuition is the state of mind which we must suppose the gods to possess. Moreover, it is in the pursuit of wisdom that we have least need of external goods or the assistance of others, and intellectual activities can be engaged in pleasantly with less admixture of pain or strain and for a longer time before fatigue sets in, than any other activity. And these are thought to be marks of happiness. For all these reasons, Aristotle concludes that the life devoted to the pursuit of wisdom is the happiest life possible for a human being. He goes on:

> Thus we should not follow the recommendation of thinkers who say that those who are human should think only of human things and that mortals should think only of mortal things, but we should try as far as possible to partake of immortality and to make every effort to live according to the best part of the soul in us; for even if this part be of small measure, it surpasses all the others by far in power and worth.

APPENDIX: THE VIRTUES AND VICES

While it is helpful to see Aristotle's list of virtues and vices laid out schematically, some of these are complicated enough that the abbreviated descriptions that fit on a chart are misleading. Consequently, I begin with narrative descriptions of each virtue, and the chart follows these.

Narrative Descriptions

Courage is moderation in the tendencies to feel fear and boldness or confidence. Excess in the propensity to fear combined with deficiency in the propensity to be confident constitutes cowardice. Deficiency of fear and excess of confidence produce rashness or foolhardiness.

Temperance is moderation in the desire for physical pleasures. An excess of desire is overindulgence. Deficiency has no common name, but may be labelled "insensitivity."

Generosity or *liberality* is moderation in the size of the gifts one is prone to give or accept. The tendency to give in excess and accept too little is spendthriftiness or prodigality. The tendency to accept too much and give too little is stinginess.

Magnificence or *munificence* has the same nature as generosity but applies to large public expenditures.

Pride or *high-mindedness* is moderation in one's desire for or tendency to demand great honors. The mean here is defined by what one deserves. Desiring more than one deserves is vanity. Desiring less than one deserves is excessive humility.

Ambition is similar to pride but pertains to smaller honors. There was no name for this virtue in Greek, and in English we use the same word both for the virtue and for the vice of excess (maybe we have trouble distinguishing them). The deficiency we just call "lack of ambition."

Good temper is moderation in one's proneness to anger. The vice of excess is irascibility or irritableness, of deficiency is spiritlessness or passivity (there's not a good word for it).

Truthfulness is what Aristotle called moderation in one's presentation of oneself, with boastfulness as the excess and self-deprecation as the deficiency.

Wittiness is moderation in the desire to amuse others. Excess desire is buffoonery, and deficient desire is boorishness.

Friendliness is moderation in the desire to please others generally. The excess is obsequiousness, and the deficiency is quarrelsomeness.

Modesty or a sense of shame is moderation in one's susceptibility to shame or embarrassment. Shyness or bashfulness is the excess, and the deficiency is shamelessness.

Righteous indignation (nemesis) is moderation in one's tendency to feel pain at the good fortune of others or pleasure at their bad fortune. Moderation consists in feeling pain at good fortune which is contrary to desert (when bad people do well), and pleasure when the good fortune is deserved. It also means feeling pain at undeserved bad fortune and pleasure when people get their comeuppance. To feel pain at all good fortune, whether deserved or not, is envy. To feel pleasure at the bad fortune of others, regardless of desert, is malice.

Justice consists in a propensity to give or return to a person the right amount (what is due to them), whereas injustice allots them either more or less than what is due. We might label the vices "favoritism" and "discrimination."

Schematic Summary

* Virtues with respect to which the chart is particularly apt to mislead are marked with an asterisk. [] Brackets enclose descriptions that don't match the columnar arrangement of the chart, or names that I have supplied for virtues or vices for which Aristotle had no name. More than one name is given when it's unclear what the best translation is.

Virtue	Relevant Passion(s)	Vice of Deficiency	Vice of Excess
*courage	boldness fear	cowardice	rashness
temperance moderation	desire for pleasure	[insensitivity]	overindulgence, intemperance
*generosity	propensity to give or accept gifts	stinginess	spendthriftiness

[Magnificence or munificence is similar to generosity, but refers only to large expenditures for public benefit.]

pride, high-mindedness	desire for large honors	excessive humility	vanity
[no common name]	desire for smaller honors	lack of ambition	ambitiousness
good temper	proneness to anger	spiritlessness	irascibility, irritability
truthfulness	self-presentation	self-deprecation	boastfulness
wittiness	desire to amuse others	boorishness	buffoonery

friendliness	desire to please others	quarrelsomeness	obsequiousness
sense of shame	susceptibility to shame	shamelessness	bashfulness, modesty
*righteous indignation	pain at good fortune of others, pleasure at their bad fortune	malice	envy

*[Justice is a mean inasmuch as it consists in a propensity to give or return to others the right amount (what is due) rather than more or less than is due.]

III

Politics

THE STATE AND THE *POLIS*

The word "politics" nowadays tends to conjure up images of political campaigns and of the arm-twisting and favor-trading that go on behind the scenes of a modern legislature. These things have a powerful influence on what government does, but they are, in an important sense, peripheral to the actual business of government. When we refer to something that happens in Washington as "politics as usual," we're insinuating that the politicians were doing something other than their proper business, or they let their proper business be influenced by something that ought not to have influenced it.

In ancient Greek, the word for "politics" referred rather to the business of government itself. Aristotle's science of politics is the science of government, the knowledge that goes with the art of governing. It doesn't give advice on how to get elected or how to push a bill through Congress. It gives advice on how to run a country.

In discussing Aristotle's political science, I will follow the same approach as in my chapter on his ethics. Rather than trying to summarize all the main points of his works on politics, I will try to acquaint the reader with what I take to be the basic standpoint from which Aristotle analyzed political life. Once you are familiar with this, it seems to me, it becomes relatively easy to turn to his own works and not only pick out but also appreciate the more specific points he is making.

The word "politics" comes from the Greek word *polis*, which is now commonly translated "state." The *polis* is the thing that the politician governs. We use the word "state" primarily to refer to a sovereign and independent political unit, subject to no higher political authority, though we also use it for political organizations whose autonomy is limited, either because they are dominated by some other state (like the states of eastern Europe during the Soviet era) or because they are members of some federal system (like the states in the United States). As the general term for a more or less independent political unit, "state" is a good translation for *polis*. It is less than ideal, however, because of certain differences between the ways we think about states and the ways the Greeks thought about the *polis*.

In the first place, when a Greek talked about a *polis*, he or she was thinking about something much smaller than the typical modern nation-state. As a piece of geography, the Greek state was less like a modern nation than like what we call a "county": a city, together with a rural area surrounding it, with perhaps some smaller towns and villages dotted about the rural area. Athens was one of the largest Greek states, but its territory was about the size of Luxembourg, or a little larger than Rhode Island. Its population probably never exceeded 350,000, and for much of its history was substantially smaller than that. And most Greek states, as I say, were even smaller. The Greeks were certainly aware of the existence of larger political units, since the forces of the Persian empire had tried to conquer them several times. And by Aristotle's day, the sovereignty of the Greek states was compromised somewhat by the domination of another centrally controlled (and in this case, feudally organized) state, the kingdom of Philip of Macedon. But they continued to exercise considerable autonomy, and apparently continued to think of the county-sized *polis* as the standard form of political organization. Aristotle's *Politics* contains no hint to the contrary.

Accordingly, if you want some idea of what an ancient Greek thought of as the normal arrangement of human political affairs, imagine yourself as living in a city of between 50,000 and 100,000 people, a city with political control over the immediately surrounding countryside; and imagine that there is no county, state, or federal government; that a majority of the world's people live in just such cities without county, state, or federal governments over them; that a journey of, say, 30 miles in any direction will take you into a different country, in most cases a country with the same language and literature as your own, but nonetheless a different country, perhaps with a repressive and tyrannical government, and above all a country in which you do not have the rights of a citizen; it may even be a country with which your country is at war. It's almost as if there were an international border every two or three exits down the interstate. And yet your fate is largely determined by the fortunes of so compact a political unit.

One reason, then, that "state" is a less than perfect translation of *polis* is that it automatically starts us thinking in terms of huge nation-states. But it also threatens to mislead us in two other ways. First, we tend to associate "state" with the apparatus of government, as distinguished from the people who are governed and from the other institutions and customs of the society. But the *polis* includes all of this. In this respect, "country" would be a better translation, for when we speak of "our country" we are referring not just to political arrangements, but to everything that characterizes, say, Americans, Mexicans, or Italians. Unfortunately, "country" shares the other shortcoming of "state," which is that we closely identify states with the territories they occupy. If some other country seized control of all our territory, we would say the United States had ceased to exist. For the Greeks, that wasn't necessarily so. During one of the Persian invasions of Greece, the Athenians actually abandoned their land and took to the sea in their very large navy. For them, this did not mean abandoning their *polis*. It meant rather that their *polis* had gone to sea. The people, organized as a political and social entity, *were* the *polis*. Their land was just the *polis*'s location. (Fortunately, they defeated the Persians at sea and got their land back.)

To a Greek, then, the "state" was not essentially a piece of territory, and it included not just the government but also the society of which the government was a part. Recognizing this, you can understand why, when Aristotle sought to identify the genus of *polis*, what he came up with was "association." The state, that is, is a kind of thing which is constituted by people associating with each other. The Greek word for "association," *koinonía*, can apply to a business partnership, a marriage, the relationship of parent and child, the relationship of master and slave, an extended family (if they live together), a village, and an alliance between nations. The word is sometimes translated as "community," but unlike the English word, it doesn't necessarily imply close emotional bonds or shared, deeply held values, though it doesn't rule them out either. It simply refers to any ongoing relationship in which something is held in common.

Aristotle's assigning the state to the genus of associations seems to me to gain credibility from the small size of the typical Greek state. That is, it is easier for me to fit a city of 50,000 into the same genus with families and villages than to do the same for a nation of 250 million.

In sum, I think that Aristotle's description of the state as a kind of association articulates what the average Greek thought (though perhaps implicitly) about the state, and in doing so, points up the respects in which this viewpoint is poorly captured by our word, "state." There is, however, no English word that translates *polis* exactly, and I shall therefore follow current usage in rendering it as "state," with the hope that the foregoing discussion will have inoculated the reader somewhat against its hazards.

WHAT THE STATE IS FOR

In discussing the shortcomings of "state" as a translation for *polis*, I have described some of the characteristics of a typical Greek state, and identified the genus to which the state belongs. Our next task is to complete the definition of "state." For the most important thing for a politician to know—the first principle of political science—is the end for which the state exists. And to know that end is also to know what the state is.

In identifying these two kinds of knowledge, Aristotle's science of politics differs from what we call political science. The modern discipline of political science studies how political institutions operate—how they are put together, what the sources of change in them are, what sorts of things make them break down, what sorts keep them going. As an empirical science, it gathers extensive data about actual governments. It sometimes predicts, or tries to predict, the consequences of different political arrangements and policies. But it begs off deciding which sets of consequences are the best. That's because it strives to be a "value-free" science.

Aristotle recognized the importance for a practicing politician of empirical data about actual states, both present and past. Before writing the *Politics*, he compiled a survey of the constitutions of 158 Greek states, and he seems to draw on that information frequently in the *Politics*. (Unfortunately, the survey itself has been lost, except for the part on Athens.) He often documents his claims about the effects of some policy by citing an incident from history, whether Greek or non-Greek. He, too, considered it part of the politician's business to understand how different forms of government originate, what sorts of causes lead to revolutions, and how different forms of government can be preserved. Much of his analysis would be right at home in a modern treatise, as for example, when he discusses the impact of different economic classes on political affairs, or makes an inventory of the offices every state must have, or classifies the functions of government as executive, legislative, and judicial. The *Politics* thus contains a great deal of historical anecdote, conceptual analysis, and practical advice that could be described as "value-free."

But Aristotle places all of this in the context of the primary job of the politician: to decide what is best for the state. His politics is thus very much a "value-laden" science. Of course, as a science, politics cannot deal with the particular decisions politicians must make in particular concrete circumstances. It can only try to provide the general principles behind such decisions. Its first task, then, is to identify the overall end of political association, and in the light of that end, to determine what form of government provides the best means for attaining it. Since politics is meant to be a practical science, the "best form of government" really refers to three different phenomena: First, there is the form that would be best if the circumstances in which the government exists—the character of the populace, the socioeconomic structure of the society, the physical characteristics of the natural environment—could be tailor-made to the politician's specifications, so that there was no obstacle to creation of the ideal state. Second, that form could be called "best" that suits the majority of actual states, in which a variety of conditions do tend to frustrate the ideal to a greater or lesser degree. Finally, there are those forms of government that would be best for various particular kinds of society one might be dealing with. All of these are legitimate topics of political science.

We might say that Aristotle's politics is more concerned with ideal governments than with real governments. But in Aristotle's world the ideal and the real are not as far apart as other thinkers suppose. To put the issue in Aristotelian terms, we should talk not about the real and the ideal, but about the relationship between nature and the good. We must understand this relationship in order to appreciate (a) how knowing the end of the state is part of

knowing what the state is, (b) how Aristotle can speak so confi-
dently about the state having an end and about the particular end
he assigns to it, and (c) how he can specify the proper job of the
politician. Discussion of that relationship will take us away from
politics for a bit, but without it one is likely to get a distorted picture of Aristotle's political science. This "digression" will also shed
further light on Aristotle's ethics and on the relationship between
ethics and politics.

Aristotle's general opinion on the relationship of nature and the
good can be stated very simply. We can talk about "the good" in
an abstract way, but we must not forget that this *is* abstract. In
reality, whatever is good must be a good *of* or *for* some subject.
What is good *for* a subject is anything that promotes the good *of*
that subject. And the good *of* a subject is the full development of
that subject's potential, the full actualization of its nature.

This is clearest (and most clearly appropriate) if we think in
biological terms. The good of an organism, biologically considered, is health. I am using the word "health" here as shorthand for
all the physical attributes we consider good—not just the absence
of disease, but such things as strength, coordination, agility, visual
acuity, and so on. Health is the condition in which the various
subsystems of which the organism is composed, and the organism
itself as the system of these systems, are functioning properly, are
functioning in the way nature "intended" them to. ("Intended"
has to be in quotes because nature, you remember, is not a reasoning being who consciously chooses to do things in certain ways; it
is a built-in principle that operates automatically, although
Aristotle seems to think its effects are the same as reason would
have chosen if it had been given the job of arranging the world.)
When your body is healthy, your nature as a biological being is in
a state of perfect actualization. In fact, we can say that the end or
final cause of life, considered in purely biological terms, is no more
or less than to be healthy. Both to avoid ambiguity and to be true
to Aristotle, perhaps we should say that the final cause of life is to
live a healthy life, that is, not just to have one's body in a certain
condition, but to engage in the kinds of activities which that condition makes possible. Within the limits of biology, that is what it
means to live well.

We don't normally talk about the good of an inorganic object,
but since the concepts of nature and of final cause apply at this

level, too, it would not be inappropriate, from an Aristotelian viewpoint, to do so. When a heavy (earthy) body such as a rock falls, that is the actualization of its nature, so it would not be as absurd as it may sound to say that it is good for it to fall, or that being at the center of the cosmos is the good of a rock. In general, to understand the nature of a thing is to understand the final cause that is programmed into it and thus governs its behavior. Its behavior is or results in the realization of that final cause, and such realization is what the good is for that thing. Hence, to know the nature of a thing and to know what is the good of that thing are really the same knowledge.

Rocks falling—or not falling—present us with a very simple system. If not supported, a rock falls. It can be prevented from falling by supporting it. Nature always operates in the same way unless something forcefully prevents it. And how nature operates, in the simple cases, is obvious to everyone.

As things get more complicated, they become less obvious. At a certain point on the ladder of evolution, organisms develop the ability to learn patterns of behavior that are not programmed into them by their genetic inheritance. In Aristotelian language, they become capable of acquiring habits. A few more notches up, and you arrive at beings whose actions are subject to an additional influence—the influence of conscious conceptions of what is best, which guide choices among alternative behaviors. These developments lead to a wide variety of behaviors among the members of a single species, that is, among animals all of whom have the same nature. So we end up attributing what is the same among them to their common nature and attributing their differences to other sources under the headings of "environment" or "nurture" or "culture." As contemporary debates about the sources of intelligence and about gender differences demonstrate, it is often difficult to determine how far our abilities and tendencies are due to our genetic endowment and how far they are due to the accidents of our life-histories. But apart from the problems involved in applying the nature-nurture distinction to particular issues, the distinction itself creates a problem for ethical and political thought.

The value-judgments we are called upon to make in the practical sciences of ethics and politics are judgments about what ways of life are best for individuals and for cities. But different ways of life involve differences in culture rather than nature. On the other hand, we have seen that the good of a thing is the fulfillment of its nature. How, then, can we extend the concept of a natural good into an area that lies outside the natural? Many people have drawn the conclusion that the only conception of the good that can be based on human nature is the biological conception of the good as health. Apart from distinguishing healthy from unhealthy lifestyles, they would claim that ways of life cannot be distinguished as better and worse. People might prefer one way of life over another, but no such preference can be justified nor disagreements decided by appeal to human nature. People want what they want, and that's about all we can say.

One alternative to that viewpoint is to find some basis for value-judgments other than the appeal to nature. Some philosophers have tried to do this, but not Aristotle. He adopts the third alternative of saying that while no way of life is natural in the sense that a human being will adopt it as inevitably as a rock will fall, there is still a way of life that can be called "natural" in the sense that it represents the optimum fulfillment of human nature.

Distinctions between nature and other sorts of causes (such as art or habit) are useful and important, but ultimately everything must be traced back to nature. Art, for example, produces objects which are not in the ordinary sense natural objects, for the cause of their production is outside themselves. But to produce objects of art is a natural function for human beings, and humans produce artifacts in order to satisfy needs and desires which they have by nature. This is why I said in discussing the four causes that it was misleading to speak of the shape of a statue as the formal cause which defined its final cause. A more adequate analysis would recognize that people make statues for a reason—Aristotle would say, to give the observers of the statues the kinds of pleasure that people naturally derive from looking at such things. The final cause of a statue (or any other work of art or craft) thus really turns out to be a purpose, and a definition of "statue" which captured the essence of what it is to be a statue by stating the formal cause of a thing's being a statue (whew!) would have to include a statement of this purpose. Statues' being shaped in various particular ways are just so many means to achieving this purpose. If you want to give a causal analysis of a particular act of sculpting, or of the sculpting of a certain genre of statues, you will have to talk about particular shapes. But if you were making an Aristotelian science of sculpture in general, your definition of a statue would refer to the purpose behind sculpting but make no mention of particular shapes. If you are going to sculpt at all, you must give your material some shape, but obviously there is no generic shape shared by all statues.

To really understand an art, then, you must identify the function its products serve relative to human nature. (And if Martians make things, you will have to identify the function their products serve relative to Martian nature.) This function serves as the standard for value-judgments about works of art, just as, in the case of a natural object, your conception of its nature is the basis for judgments about what is good for it. A good human being, in Aristotle's view, is one whose life most perfectly expresses what it means to be a human being. A good artifact is one that performs well the function it is best suited to serve in contributing to the achievement of the human good.

This kind of analysis applies to all "non-natural" products and activities. Habitual behaviors, including the habits we call virtues and vices, are not natural, inasmuch as we do not spontaneously and inevitably develop particular habits. They are natural, however, in two senses: First, we do naturally acquire some habits. That is, our nature does not dictate specifically what habits we shall acquire; that is determined by a number of variables, including chance. But we are so constituted by nature that in the course of interacting with our environments, we tend to repeat behaviors that seem to work, until they become habitual, automatic, second-nature. We are, so to speak, habit-forming animals, and it is in our nature to be so. Second, the behaviors that become habitual represent ways of satisfying natural needs and desires. Cultivating crops, for example, can hardly be said to be part of human nature, since a great many human beings lived out their lives before agriculture was invented, and societies that do not practice agriculture still exist. Nonetheless, agriculture is natural in the sense that it is one of the ways of satisfying our natural need for food.

What it comes down to is this: To understand anything that people make or do, you have to understand why they make or do it. That means you have to identify the natural need or desire which the product or activity helps to satisfy. Human behaviors vary from culture to culture (and even from individual to individual) because there are different ways of satisfying these needs and desires. Some of these differences don't make any difference with respect to satisfying the need in question. But other differences can make a difference. Some activities, habits, or ways of life may be more effective than others in satisfying our needs; some of them may lead to more adequate satisfactions than others; some may do a better job of satisfying one need at minimal cost in terms of the frustration of other needs. Again, if we revert to the biological domain, these points are fairly clear. Human diets vary widely. Some differences in diet don't represent a difference in nutritional value: you can have two quite different but equally nutritious diets. But we also regularly distinguish between better and worse diets, and we can do this on several grounds. Some diets fail to supply the basic nutrients. Some diets supply what we need but are "inefficient" either because their ingredients are difficult or expensive to obtain or prepare, or because their concentrations of nutrients are so low that we would have to eat a great deal to get our daily requirements, or because they are hard to digest. Finally, some diets supply the necessary nutrients but frustrate other needs, either by being unhealthy in other ways (containing pesticides, carcinogens, cholesterol), or by being unappetizing. In every case, the standard by which we judge diets as better or worse is their success or failure in satisfying (and not frustrating) the set of natural needs and desires on which they have an impact.

Aristotle thought all of our activities can be seen as ways of trying to fulfill our natural potentialities. And accordingly they can be judged with respect to how well they do this. Notice one important consequence of looking at things this way. The purpose of human actions is given by human nature. But the specific actions in which you engage are a result not only of this nature but also of your previous experience, the habits you have developed, and your own understanding of your nature and desires. That means that the natural purpose for which you engage in an action may be different from the purpose you are consciously aware of. In fact, since I earlier resolved to use the term "purpose" only for conscious intentions, perhaps I should stop speaking of our natural purposes. Strictly speaking, what our nature gives us is ends. Both our conscious purposes and our habits derive from these, but our habits may represent flawed means of pursuing these ends, and our conscious purposes may distort them.

The purpose of ethical thought is to overcome the distortions that have grown up over time and identify what our nature truly is, and thereafter to determine what instruments and ways of life make possible or represent the most efficient and most adequate fulfillment of that nature. If someone wants to know why humans do a certain kind of thing, an answer in terms of the agents' conceptions of their motives and the agents' habits is only partial. A complete answer must trace the action back to its "real" motives, its sources in human nature. And a final judgment on the desirability of a kind of instrument or way of life must be made not in terms of its success in satisfying the perceived needs of its users or practitioners, but in the light of its success in fulfilling the potentialities really present in human nature.

What has all this to do with politics? The job of the politician is to govern a state. A state is a kind of association. Associations generally and states in particular are things that people make. We make them by entering into them and participating in them. Consequently, the way we must understand the state is similar to that in which we understand artifacts and habits. We must figure out what the function of a state is. Participating in a state is a way of satisfying certain human needs, a way of promoting the fulfillment of some aspects of human nature. When we know what these are, we will understand the "nature" of a state.

We create political offices in states so that there will be people responsible for seeing to it that the functions of the state are performed, and performed well. That is the politician's job. The most important thing for a politician to know, then, is what the state is for. To know that function is both to know what a state essentially is and to be in possession of the standard for assessing particular arrangements and policies within the state—for making the value-judgments that guide the politician's decisions.

All of the ends that human beings have by nature, and hence all of the ends that lie behind human making and doing, can be subsumed under the term "happiness." A happy life is one in which all of these ends receive their optimal fulfillment, taking into account their relative importance. To ask what states are for is therefore equivalent to asking what parts of human happiness the state is designed to serve.

As Aristotle defined it in the *Nicomachean Ethics*, "happiness" refers primarily to the fulfillment of the distinctively human aspects of human beings. He makes it something like the health of the human soul. "Activity of soul in accord with virtue" is equivalent to "the good functioning of the human being qua human, the most perfect actualization of those aspects of the soul that are peculiarly human." But since we are also animals, and therefore by nature share certain traits with other animals, our nature includes other than specifically human potentialities. Aristotle therefore includes the fulfillment of these potentialities as subordinate components in a larger conception of happiness. This larger conception thus includes what he calls the goods of the body, or what I earlier called "health" in a broad sense of the term. Further, the fulfillment of both our specifically human and our generically animal needs requires some quantity of material possessions, so Aristotle includes these, too, under the title of "external goods." The old educational ideal of "a sound mind in a sound body" is a thoroughly Aristotelian notion, and Aristotle would add "a sound bank account" into the equation. At the same time, we must not forget that the acquisition of virtue, and especially of intellectual virtue, is the most important ingredient in human well-being.

What contribution can the state make to the achievement of happiness? In answering this question, we must recall something I said earlier about the Greek conception of the *polis*. The *polis* is not the apparatus of government as distinguished from other aspects of society. The term refers properly to the association of people in a state—their interacting with each other in certain ways, their sharing their lives to a certain extent. The apparatus that governs this shared life is only a part of it. When you begin to think of the state this way, it becomes evident that it is not simply one association among others. It incorporates all smaller associations into it. It becomes the context within which families, friendships, and partnerships operate. To what extent government regulates these smaller associations is a variable, but they are all affected directly or indirectly by legislation. And they are all profoundly affected by customs and ways of thought that are not legislated but tend to become uniform throughout the society, throughout the *polis*. Aristotle is serious about putting the *polis* at the next step on a scale of size and complexity after the family and the village. The *polis* is us living together, with a very large "us." To ask what contribution the state can make to happiness is therefore not the same as the question, What should government do for the people?

It is really the question, What benefits can people derive from living in a society large enough to qualify as a state?

Since the state includes all smaller associations, I think the best way to answer this is to talk about the benefits of association generally, rather than just thinking about states in particular. Later, I can pinpoint what it is that distinguishes the state from other associations.

The ways in which association with others affects our possibilities for obtaining external goods are familiar to us. Politicians' speeches may talk a lot about noneconomic values, whether they are called "spiritual," "democratic," or "family" values. But when we start debating actual courses of action, most of the talk seems to revolve around money. It may be worthwhile, then, to make a quick survey of the entire range of human interests on which association has an impact. Following Aristotle's lead, let's divide these into external goods, the goods of the body, and the goods of the soul.

The first benefit of association is that it enables us to protect ourselves better from predators, whether human or nonhuman, and to better defend ourselves against the destructive forces of nature. It thus gives us increased security in the possession of every sort of good. Second come the benefits economists like to talk about. Cooperation, especially over the long term, makes specialization possible. I will make shoes, you will make shirts, he will build furniture, and she will farm, and then we will trade the products of our labor. One result of this arrangement is that the shoes, shirts, furniture, and vegetables that "we" produce are better than the ones we would have if each of us tried to make everything for him- or herself.

Economic cooperation increases the variety and quality of the external possessions available to us. It also makes it possible for individuals to amass a greater quantity of possessions than is possible in the absence of political association; specialization and exchange enable individuals to acquire more property, and the security provided by the political system enables them to continue in the possession of it.

Association also enhances our ability to pursue the goods of body and soul, and in two ways. First, the goods of body and soul are indirectly affected by the impact of association on external goods.

The goods of the body are enhanced by improved diet, facilities and equipment for physical training, medical technology, and increasing control over the environment. Intellectual goods are enhanced by the availability of physical facilities and apparatus for education and research. Perhaps less obvious, because we tend to take it for granted, is the role of economic development in creating leisure time, which is the prerequisite for intense intellectual work. You probably don't think of academic work as a leisure pastime. It is strenuous and demanding. But we can only devote time to intellectual pursuits if we can spare the time from the task of securing the necessities of life. A society does not need to be far along the road of economic development to be able to support genuine specialists in the pursuit of knowledge. But you can imagine how almost impossible intellectual progress would be for someone who lived apart from society.

The economic benefits of cooperation affect the other goods of the soul, the ethical goods, in two ways. First, there are certain virtues that obviously depend on one's living well above the subsistence level. Generosity is only possible if you have some property to spare. And if you are to demonstrate courage in its most dramatic form, by participation in battle, you must have arms, which in most Greek states the soldier was expected to provide at his own expense. Second, Aristotle believed that the fullest development of the ethical virtues, no less than of the intellectual, depended on the possession of leisure. Many of the virtues find their fullest development in activities not immediately directed toward making a living, and consequently only those who are freed from the constant pursuit of the necessities of life are able to participate in these activities. Aristotle in fact believed that people like carpenters and shoemakers could not become truly virtuous because their occupations were not in themselves conducive to the development of virtue, and they did not leave the workers the free time or the means to participate in activities that do develop the virtues.

One way, then, that association with others affects the goods of body and soul is indirect, through its effect on external possessions. But there are also more direct effects. The goods of the body are enhanced by having other people around who will play with us, compete with us, and coach us. The ethical virtues are enhanced by living with people who will raise us in good habits as children and reinforce us in those habits as adults. And the intel-

lectual virtues benefit from association with people who will in-
struct us in the arts and sciences and cooperate with us in research
aimed at enlarging our collective knowledge.

Beyond this, association with others is a precondition for exercising many of the ethical virtues, quite apart from the economic
prerequisites they may have. If you look again at the narrative
descriptions of the virtues and vices in the appendix to the previous chapter, you will see that most of them involve our relationships to other people. You can't be generous without someone to
be generous to. Evenness of temper is moderation in one's tendency to become angry, but the most significant potential objects
of our anger are other people. Pride or "high-mindedness" is defined not with reference to a private feeling of importance, but in
terms of a propensity to demand certain kinds of honor for oneself—honor, of course, from other people. Even courage bears a
reference to other people, for in the paradigm case of courage, that
shown by a soldier in battle, the danger comes from other people
and is endured on behalf of one's fellow-citizens.

The ethical virtue most intimately connected to association with
others is one the Greeks called *philia*. This word, usually translated
"friendship," covers the entire range of relationships characterized by a feeling of solidarity between the people involved, from
the closest friendship to the kind of fellow-feeling that arises
among people flying on the same airplane. The disposition to enter into such relationships—friendliness—is a virtue, especially in
its purest form as a readiness to become best friends with a person
whose virtue makes him or her worthy of admiration and love.

The conclusion seems to be, then, not that associating with others can provide us with all the ingredients of happiness, but that it
has a significant contribution to make in every department of happiness. That contribution is large enough, in fact, that without
participating in associations, we could not be completely happy—
in fact, we would be quite far from it.

But the question recurs, Where does the state fit into all this? In
order to answer this question, we have to figure out what distinguishes the state from other associations. The most obvious feature of the state, as distinguished from an extended family or a
village, is its size. But at what point does a village become big
enough to qualify as a state? Aristotle's answer is very simple. An
association becomes a state when it becomes big enough to be self-

sufficient; that means, big enough that all the needs of human nature can be adequately satisfied within it. The state must be big enough to make possible the kind of division of labor that enables it to produce external goods of high quality in ample quantities. It must produce the necessities of life efficiently enough that there is leisure time left over for the cultivation of the excellences of body and soul. If the realization of human potential is to be maximized, there must be specialists in physical, mental, and moral education. And those who are capable of extraordinary achievements must be freed from the menial tasks of life to pursue their higher callings.

Aristotle does not try to pin down a particular size of population or territory as the minimum for a state. His point is rather that when people advance beyond the simplest forms of association, they do so in the hope of attaining a more complete happiness. Hence the progress from smaller to larger associations finds its consummation—its end—in an association capable of contributing all that associations can to the happiness of their members. This becomes in effect both the definition of the state and the answer to the question, What does the state contribute to human happiness? Since the state is an association which incorporates all smaller associations into it, their contributions to happiness become parts of its contribution. Again, this only makes sense if you keep thinking of the state as the society, not the government. Consider how many of the activities through which you seek to live a good life are also at the same time ways of participating in United States society, or in the various smaller associations that are a part of it (which include your family and your circle of friends). This is not to say that you couldn't pursue happiness equally well in some other society, even in a very different society. But surely it would be incredible to suppose you could achieve happiness, understood as the fullest development of your potential, apart from all association with other persons. And since the state is defined precisely as an association which is capable of supplying all that association can supply to human need, it follows that it is impossible for a human being to be happy who does not live in a state.

Turning that around, we can say that the function of the state, the purpose for which we create states, is to promote the happiness of us, their members. This does not mean that the first people to organize themselves into states had a sophisticated understanding of happiness or were aware of all the potential benefits of this new level of organization. Aristotle himself says, "The state came into existence for the sake of living, but exists for the sake of living well." I take this to mean that the first organizers of states may have seen them only as vehicles for cooperation in securing the necessities of life and in protecting themselves from aggression. But having come together for these reasons, they later discovered that the political association offered other benefits as well. In fact, it made possible ways of life in which one could enjoy happiness of a different order than anything available in simpler societies. A richer conception of happiness grew up in the same social context that made the pursuit of that kind of happiness possible. And of course, a definitive account of happiness had to wait on the genius of an Aristotle. Nonetheless, even that definitive account is only a spelling out of what was already implicit in the first human impulse toward association, or toward action at all, however poorly the first city-dwellers understood it.

Aristotle is often quoted as referring to the human being as a "political animal," but I'm not sure people are always clear about what this means. I think it means three things. First, we are equipped by nature with the prerequisites for participating in political associations. We have reason, which enables us to deliberate about courses of action; we have language, which enables us to do this together with other people; and we have a sense of good and bad, and of just and unjust, which goes beyond a reflex reaction to pleasure and pain—and Aristotle suggests that a common understanding of such values is a necessary ingredient in a state. Second, we are naturally gregarious. We have a natural tendency to enter into associations, and since this naturally culminates in the ultimate association, the state, we can be said to have a natural impulse toward forming states. Finally, and most importantly, there is the point made above, that complete happiness can only be found in a state. But happiness is identical with the most perfect expression of human nature. Hence, the primary sense in which human beings are political animals is that we are the kind of animals whose nature is only fully expressed through participation in a political association. Only in such a context can our lives fully illustrate what it means to be human. Aristotle is so convinced of this that he says that anyone who lived outside the state not because of contingent circumstances (like being marooned on a desert island) but because of his or her nature would have to be either an evil and savage sort of creature (like the cyclops that attacked Odysseus) or something far better than a human being, like a god. The former is not fit to associate with others, and the latter does not need them.

Many people in our day and age are made uncomfortable by the suggestion that some people's lives are better expressions of what it means to be human than others'. It only makes matters worse to add that the better lives can be attributed to living in better societies. And when the distinction between better and worse societies is made to parallel that between larger, more complex and smaller, simpler societies, many people will be prompted to outraged protest. I don't know if it will help any to point out that Aristotle was incapable of comparing life in a small isolated village (it would have to be isolated, because a village that is part of a larger state would make for a false comparison) to life in a modern industrial society, undergirded by modern technology and plagued by the dangers technology has brought in its train, and burdened also by the social dislocations and psychological stresses for which modern life is famous. In fact, he seems not to have thought it possible for anything as big as a modern nation to form a single state. If he could make such a comparison, perhaps he would have preferred the village. But comparing the typical Greek *polis* to the isolated village, he felt no doubt that the former was a better environment for human flourishing than the latter. That will be enough to condemn him in the eyes of those who insist that the simplest kind of tribal life could leave nothing to be desired in the way of genuine happiness.

The issue is a complicated one, and entering into debate about it would take us too far away from the exposition of Aristotle's thought. But I would like to say just a few words on Aristotle's behalf. His judgments about simpler societies and his judgments about better and worse states at the same level are not based on mere prejudice. He felt that it was a matter for scientific inquiry to determine what sorts of arrangements were most conducive to human happiness. He just thought it was pretty obvious to a neutral observer that a state on the order of Athens or Thebes or Corinth offered more opportunities for personal development than a small village. And when you put it that way, I certainly couldn't disagree with it. When it comes to comparing different states of similar size but with different constitutions, laws, and customs, it will be less obvious which is superior. And it won't necessarily be the case that one will be superior to another. Each system may have its own advantages and disadvantages, and these might cancel each other out. Besides, as I said earlier, not every difference has to make a difference in terms of the impact on human happiness. Nonetheless, some differences surely do make a difference. And everyone who prefers one social policy or custom to another is implicitly saying that a state which followed that policy or custom would be better (other things being equal) than one that didn't. The idea that some societies are better than others thus seems to be implicit in the act of political decision-making. To choose one course of action over another is to make your society into one kind rather than another.

THE FORMS OF GOVERNMENT

We have now arrived at an answer to the question, What is the state for? The function of the state is to promote the happiness of the people. That's the first thing the politician needs to know. The second is what happiness is. So every politician should make a thorough study of Aristotle's ethics before embarking on his or her career. The next job after that is to identify in a general way the political arrangements that are most conducive to this end. "In a general way," because decisions on particular matters require a judgment call, and so must be left to the prudence of the politician.

The fundamental political arrangement in a society is what we call its "form of government." The politician needs to know what form of government is the best, since his or her actions will be guided to some extent by this ideal. But politics, like other practical sciences, is not just concerned with knowing how to operate under ideal conditions. It must also know how to make the best of whatever the practitioner is given to start with. Most politicians are not founders of states; they are born into a state which already has some form of government, and it will probably be other than the best. And both the founder of a state and the politician who finds him or herself in an existing state must deal with some particular population, with its own capabilities, customs, and values, and with some particular territory, with its own possibilities and limitations regarding natural resources, defensibility, proximity of friendly or hostile neighbors, and so on. The politician, therefore, needs to know what form of government is best relative to various circumstances. It will also be helpful here, as in other arts, to know what sort of thing works most of the time in most circumstances. Finally, it belongs to the same science to understand both the good and the bad with respect to its subject matter. So the political scientist must study all the forms of government and their relative merits and demerits.

Our government textbooks sometimes divide governments into monarchies, aristocracies, and democracies, according to whether one person, a few people, or everyone excercises political power. Aristotle's classification is more complicated. In the first place, he recognizes that the *proportion* of the society that excercises power is less important than what *kind* of people they are. A society governed by wealthy merchants concerned primarily with economic prosperity will differ in significant ways from one governed by land-owning nobles with a tradition of aristocratic values, even though both these ruling classes represent wealthy minorities. Moreover, there are a number of variables in the distribution of power in a society. If eligibility for office is highly restricted, but the right to vote in elections is widely extended, we seem to have a hybrid form. Again, different powers may be assigned to different segments of society. For example, declarations of war and other military matters may be the exclusive prerogative of a small senate or council of elders, while issues related to trade and manufacture are decided by an assembly of all the citizens. Finally, particular measures tend to encourage or reinforce a particular distribution of power, often independently of the official, legally established form of government. To use one of Aristotle's own examples, you may have a government which is officially a pure democracy, with all legislation being voted on by a citizen assembly. But if you impose a fine on the wealthy for failure to attend the assembly, and do not impose a fine on the poorer people (because paying the fine would be too great a burden and they may more urgently need to attend to their own business), you in fact are encouraging the wealthy minority to participate in government and the less prosperous majority to voluntarily disenfranchise themselves. The more such measures you enact, the less democratic your democracy is.

Aristotle tries to take all of these variables into account. Nonetheless, the basic framework of his classification corresponds, with one radical difference, to the classification we are familiar with. There is a similarity because, while our classification is based on the number of people who hold power and his on the particular class or group that holds power, there is almost always a correlation between these two variables. The wealthy are almost always a minority, the poor or the middle class, or both together, a majority. The radical difference between Aristotle's classification and ours is that he makes a distinction which gives him six basic forms of government instead of three. Aristotle recognized that not every state is run in such a way as to pursue the proper end of the state. Some forms of government represent perversions of or deviations from good government. A classification corresponding to the class or number of people who hold power must therefore be subdivided according to whether the government is aiming at its proper end.

Let's go into a little more detail about what that means. The political association is created and sustained by those who participate in it. It derives its end from those people, to whom it stands as an instrument for promoting their happiness. In the nature of the case, then, the state is meant to promote the happiness of *all* the citizens. The political good, Aristotle says, is the same as the common interest, and is also identical with what is just. But many governments are organized so as to serve the interests of only a part of the society. This is not to say that any government can totally ignore the interests of the majority of its citizens. But in many governments, the interests of part of the society are completely subordinated to those of some other part. In such a society, some of those who ought to be citizens are being treated instead as slaves. For it is characteristic of a slave-owner to be concerned for the interests of the slave only to the extent that it is necessary to further the master's own interests. A prudent master may recognize that fostering a certain level of contentment in the slaves is a more effective way of preventing rebellion and getting good work out of them than constant threats and punishments. That does not alter the fundamental fact that the slave is a piece of property and that only the master is granted the status of a full-fledged human being.

The first division of governments, then, is into good governments, which pursue the common good, and bad governments, which function primarily as instruments of exploitation. Within each of these divisions is a threefold classification which corresponds to the number of people who hold political power. But as I said earlier, the number of people who hold power is less important than which class or segment of society is in control, and this is particularly true with respect to the classification of a government as good or bad. That is, whether a society is good or bad is not determined by whether it is governed by one, a few, or the many, but by what kind of person the one is, which minority holds power, or what the character of the many is and how they are organized.

A single person given absolute authority because he or she excels all others in virtue would work for the common good, and the government of such a person is a kingship or a *monarchy*. A selfish person, concerned more with his or her own pleasure than with nobility of conduct, would, if he or she won total authority, create a *tyranny* and exploit all others as far as possible. (The Greek word *monarchia* just meant "rule by one," and Aristotle applies it to both tyranny and what I am calling monarchy. His word for the good form is usually translated "kingship," but really means "king-or-queenship," because he could use the same word regardless of the monarch's gender. But we don't have a word like that, so I'm pressing "monarch" into service as a nongender-specific term for the good form of rule by one person.)

When government is bestowed on a number of persons because of their outstanding virtue, they too will rule with a view to the common interest, and their government is called *aristocracy*, which means "rule by the best." Aristocracy had to be government by a minority, on Aristotle's view, because only a minority of people are capable of attaining the full range of virtues. The qualification for governing, other than virtue, that almost always produces government by a minority is wealth. When a substantial amount of property is made a precondition of participation, government tends to be dominated by people who care for their own financial welfare more than anything else, and the public interest is systematically subordinated to the interests of this class. Such a government is called an *oligarchy*. (The word "oligarchy" orginally just meant "government by a few," but in Aristotle's day and ever since it has been taken to mean "government by the wealthy," usually with the implication that it is also government for the benefit of the wealthy.)

When participation in government is extended to everyone— well, here we must insert certain qualifications. For purposes of classifying governments, "everyone" doesn't mean literally everyone. Children and foreigners are naturally excluded. In ancient Greece, as in most societies before the twentieth century, all women were excluded. Moreover, slavery was widespread in ancient Greece, and slaves, of course, had no political rights. The third and broadest level of participation in government was therefore represented by a system in which every free adult male citizen had a voice. This group naturally constituted less than a majority of the total membership of society, in fact, less than a majority of the total adult membership of society.

When government is extended to "everyone," it tends to be dominated by those relatively lacking in material resources, since these are almost always the majority in any society. These people tend to be wrapped up in improving their lot in life, and will see government primarily as a vehicle for bettering their condition at the expense of the rich. Government by "all" which serves not the common interest but the selfish interests of the poorer classes was referred to by Aristotle as *democracy* (rule by the people). His use of this term for an essentially bad form of government may take some getting used to.

The good form of government by all Aristotle calls by the Greek term *politeia*. This label for one particular form of government is also the word for "form of government" in general. It seems impossible to find a single English word that will serve for both the wider and the narrower senses of this term, and for the narrower sense by itself a variety of translations has been offered. Perhaps the safest course is just to skirt the issue by sticking to the Greek term.

The relationship between *politeia* and democracy is unlike that between monarchy and tyranny or that between aristocracy and oligarchy. Where power is held by one or a few, allegiance to the common interest is secured by seeing to it that the ruler or rulers are people of virtue. Presumably their commitment to noble actions, their sense of justice, and their feeling of solidarity (*philia*) with their fellow citizens will prevent them from exploiting others. When power is extended to the many, Aristotle does not feel that he can rely on virtue as a safeguard, because he thinks the majority of people are limited in their ability to acquire virtue. The solution here, he thinks, is to balance democratic features of the constitution and laws with oligarchic measures, measures designed to ensure that the interests of the minority are not neglected. For example, whereas oligarchies impose a fine on the wealthy if they refuse to serve as jurors, and democracies compensate the needy for their jury duty, a *politeia* will do both. Where democracies set no property qualification for voting in the citizen assembly (or require only a small amount of property—another way that the scope of "the people" can be limited in a democracy), and oligarchies require a large amount of property for participation, a *politeia* will require a moderate amount. Again, where democracies often choose officials by lot, with no property qualification for office, while oligarchies establish a property qualification and choose among the qualified candidates by voting, a *politeia* might choose officials by voting but without the property qualification. These are just three examples Aristotle gives of how *politeia* represents a blend of democracy and oligarchy.

Deciding which of these forms a particular government has is not always easy, and the line between *politeia* and democracy is particularly difficult to draw. The situation is made more difficult by the fact that under each of the six generic forms Aristotle identifies a number of species, and some of these species get close to the border between generic forms. Some of the species of monarchy, for example, differ only a little from some species of tyranny, especially if the tyrant happens to follow Aristotle's advice on one way to make a tyranny last, namely, to make it as much like a monarchy as possible. But we may leave these subtleties to those who wish to delve further into Aristotle's politics by wrestling with the original.

The Best Form of Government

What then is the best form of government? The best form is the one that best enables its citizens to lead a happy life. To lead a happy life, the citizens must be adequately supplied with external goods and they must be healthy and virtuous. The securing of external goods depends to a large extent on good luck. The goods of the body and the soul depend more on the natural endowments and upbringing of the citizens, and on social institutions that reinforce the results of their endowment and upbringing. If we assume a state well-provided with the goods of fortune and having a populace endowed by nature with a disposition suitable for the acquisition of virtue—in other words, if we assume that the raw materials for establishing a state are all one could wish for—then the best state, Aristotle says, would be an aristocracy. An aristocracy is ruled by the most virtuous among its citizens, and these are the most able to make prudent decisions and the most disposed to pursue the common good. With the most virtuous people in charge, the state will be best-ordered both with respect to the acquisition of external goods and with respect to the cultivation of virtue in the citizens.

If you could dictate the conditions in which a state is to be established, aristocracy would be the best form of government. But the conditions in most actual states are not amenable to the formation of an aristocracy. Aristotle felt that the form of government most likely to succeed—both to remain true to the real purpose of the state and to survive—in the conditions existing in most states was *politeia*. As a blend of oligarchic and democratic measures, *politeia* was most likely to keep the greatest number of people from all social classes satisfied with their form of government, and that is the best guarantee of stability in government. This is especially true if the society's middle class is large relative to the higher and lower classes, so Aristotle advised politicians to encourage the growth of the middle class.

If you specify particular conditions, other forms of government become the-best-under-the-circumstances. Even the bad forms of government seem appropriate, or at least the most likely to endure, given certain kinds of population to be ruled. To take an extreme example, Aristotle thought the subjects of the despotically governed Persian empire were of a naturally servile disposition, so presumably he considered tyranny the right form of government for them.

One sign of the practical intent of Aristotle's political science is that he surveys not only the conditions in which each form of government is likely to arise and the causes of the downfall of each form, but also the measures whereby the status quo can be preserved in each form, including even the bad forms. There are places in the *Politics* where you might almost think you are reading Machiavelli. But that impression never lasts long, for the entire work is informed not only by Aristotle's explicit convictions about the proper ends of government, but also by his own nobility of character. For example, he says that there are two basic methods for a tyrant to stay in power. One consists of all the oppressive measures we usually associate with the name "tyranny." The other consists in imitating monarchical government in everything except surrendering absolute power (for if that were surrendered, the government would have become a monarchy). Aristotle never says that such a benevolent dictatorship would be better than the more oppressive version, but it can hardly be doubted that his sympathies would lie in that direction.

Another sign of Aristotle's practical orientation is that when he describes the state that would be best under "ideal" conditions, his "ideal" conditions are not the best one could possibly imagine. Rather, they are the best one could reasonably hope for, given the facts about human nature and the constraints under which Aristotle thought any society would have to operate. They are the best conditions that are really possible within these limits, and even these modest ideals are, he believed, rarely encountered in actual states. His ideal state is by no means a heavenly kingdom, and many would balk at calling it a utopia. Indeed, Aristotle's views about the conditions under which any really possible state would have to operate, combined with his conviction that the highest function of a state was to instill virtue in its citizens, led him to espouse a kind of government that modern egalitarian thinkers find reprehensible.

The idea that the best state is one governed by good people is perhaps an easy one to accept. But then, we think of ordinary, decent, law-abiding citizens as good people. Except for the few who are deliberately wicked, everyone is a good person. And of good persons, anyone who is of age and mentally competent has a right to participate in government, at least to the extent of voting.

Aristotle, however, did not see it that way. In the first place, his idea of a good person was not someone who is well-intentioned and basically decent. His good person was one who had fully developed the full range of ethical and intellectual virtues, or was on the way to doing so. And he recognized two conditions which would disable a person from being a good person in this sense.

First, Aristotle thought there were people who were constitutionally incapable of guiding their own conduct through rational deliberation. They were like lower animals in that their lives, if they were left to themselves, would be dominated entirely by the nonrational, passionate, and appetitive part of their souls. His description of these people seems to fit those whom we would describe as "not competent to manage their own affairs." We put people in this category if their mental capacities are so meager that they are incapable of deliberation, or if their thought processes are disordered, or if their deliberations, of whatever quality, seem to have no effect on their conduct. People whose behavior is pathologically irrational, impulsive, and irresponsible come under this description. If these are the people Aristotle is talking about, we would agree with him that they have no business participating in government. (I assume only a really hard-core libertarian would insist that a sufferer from uncontrolled schizophrenia has a right to vote.)

Unfortunately, Aristotle's conception of mental incompetence does not quite coincide with ours, as evidenced by the fact that he used it as a justification for the institution of slavery. Aristotle said that a person who was naturally incapable of governing his or her own conduct was by nature a slave. Since these people could not regulate their behavior themselves, someone else had to do it for them. A natural slave naturally needs a master. Lacking adequate rational equipment, a slave cannot acquire genuine virtue and therefore cannot be happy in the truest sense of the term, but the slave is capable of a modified sort of virtue and a modified sort of happiness if he or she has a good master to supply the guidance his or her own intellect cannot provide.

So far we are not too far from our own notion that people who are mentally incompetent must have guardians. But Aristotle seems to take it for granted that society will be well stocked with natural slaves. He seems to believe that a relatively large proportion of the population fits into this category. But the people we classify as incompetent are a very small percentage of the population. And the level of mental disability in ancient Greece cannot have been that much higher than it is today. This makes me think that Aristotle must have been drawing the line between competent and incompetent at a much higher level than we would. Many aristocrats and would-be aristocrats in all ages have thought of the peasants and the "rabble" as lacking all sense of nobility and decorum, and totally incapable of controlling their appetites. At best they are capable of acquiring habits of humility and obedience under the close supervision of the better people. They are capable, that is, of becoming properly servile, and thus of providing good service. Something of this attitude can be seen in the movie *Remains of the Day*, in a scene in which the guests of a British lord try to demonstrate to him that his butler has neither the interest nor the ability to discuss the moving issues of contemporary politics.

I can't help suspecting that Aristotle shared a similar viewpoint, that he would regard as incompetent to participate in government a great number of people who are neither intellectually impaired nor mentally disturbed, but just not very bright and not very reliable. These people, he would say, are better off being told what to do by brighter, more reliable people.

But this is not the worst of it. To use this conception of "incompetence" to justify slavery is not simply to say that some people are better off taking orders from others. For one feature of the institution of slavery is that the interests of the slave are totally subordinated to those of the master. Indeed, the master and the master's society are concerned for the interests of the slave only insofar as taking care of the slave enables the slave to better serve the interests of the master. The slave is allowed no legitimate interests independent of the master's. This is radically different from our notion of the relationship between the mentally incompetent and their guardians. The latter is more like the relationship between parent and child. Aristotle's natural slave is treated not like a child, but like a domestic animal. The rationale for this arrangement seems to be that as one who is not capable of becoming fully happy, the natural slave is not fully human, and therefore has no claim on the legal and moral status afforded complete human beings.

At least Aristotle recognized that not every slave is a natural slave. He seems to have thought that to forcibly enslave someone not a natural slave, as was common with prisoners of war in his day, was neither just nor a good idea. Moreover, he did expect the relationship between a natural slave and his or her master to be mutually beneficial in practice, even though in principle the interests of the slave were always vulnerable to sacrifice. But in the final analysis there is no getting around the fact that he believed some people were naturally inferior to others, precisely in those features that make human beings human.

Some people, then, are by nature incapable of complete and genuine virtue. To make matters worse, there are others whose natures might admit of such flourishing, but whose ways of life prevent the development of virtue and hence of full humanness. And this was not something Aristotle thought susceptible to change.

The virtues are things that have to be cultivated. The primary arenas in which they are cultivated are warfare, scientific inquiry, and social life, including especially political activity. Participation in such activities is hampered if all or nearly all one's waking hours are spent in procuring the necessities of life, whether for oneself or for others, or if the work one devotes to procuring the necessities leaves one with little energy for engaging in character-building activities. This is what I think Aristotle means when he says that leisure—freedom from business—is necessary for the development of virtue.

Some occupations leave one little or no leisure, and yet they are occupations that no society can do without. Hence, even in the best possible society there will be people whose work prevents them from becoming fully virtuous and who therefore must be excluded from participation in government. Aristotle placed farmers—not landowners necessarily, but the people who actually work the land—in this class.

Artisans and laborers suffer from the same handicap, and another as well. Aristotle describes their way of life as "ignoble and inconsistent with virtue." It is widely recognized that Aristotle and the Greeks generally had a low opinion of manual labor. It is sometimes implied that they thought it was demeaning to get your hands dirty, like Chinese mandarins who grew long fingernails to show that they didn't work with their hands. I think this misrepresents Aristotle (I don't know about the mandarins). In the first place, many of these occupations were unpleasant in themselves, especially in the days of primitive technology. The work of wage-laborers was often almost literally back-breaking. The blacksmith's forge and the tanner's vats did not provide the most ideal working environment. To have to engage in unpleasant work tends to break a person's spirit. It's humiliating. But I suspect that an even stronger reason for Aristotle's attitude is that the people who work in these professions are constantly at the beck and call of other people. The crafts-worker is always trying to keep the customer satisfied. The wage-laborer is at the mercy of the boss. (They didn't have unions in those days.) The social conditions in which these people work thus demand of them a certain measure of servility, of "slave-like" behavior. This is antithetical to the concept of the virtuous person as self-sufficient, self-governing, and proud.

It is hard for us, with our modern technology and our egalitarian principles, to see Aristotle's attitude as anything other than class-prejudice. In fairness to Aristotle, I think we must recognize that there are kinds of work and conditions of labor that tend to stunt one's mind and one's body, and to warp one's character. If Aristotle could not envision a society in which everyone was freed from the necessity to engage in that kind of work, we should not be too quick to decide that this represented a failure of imagination on his part, rather than an acknowledgment of the real limits of possibility at a certain level of technical and social development.

Whatever our final verdict on the matter, the fact remains that Aristotle excluded farmers, artisans, and laborers from participation in the government of his ideal society. The business of governing is thus assigned to a class of people who are free, wealthy, and virtuous. In their youth, they form the military element in the society, or at least the core of it, perhaps like the medieval knighthood. As they get older, they assume political leadership of the society. Even in an aristocracy, the principle of rule by the majority is recognized, but the "majority" in this case is the majority of aristocrats.

One feature of this aristocracy is that it has its priorities right. It regards the inculcation of virtue (in those capable of it by nature and occupation) as more important than tending to the external goods of the society. Hence, the most important job of the rulers is to oversee the system of education which will produce virtuous citizens. Aristotle began what promised to be a lengthy treatment of the form this education should take, but either he never finished it or the latter part of it has been lost. I won't go into it here, except to say that it is interesting to compare that part of the *Politics* to Plato's *Republic*, another work on the best state which is devoted largely to a discussion of education. Taking a clue from that work, we may presume that Aristotle expected the education system to be the guarantor that people would be admitted into political power on the basis of merit rather than that of noble ancestry or wealth. In other words, I think both philosophers would give the same answer to the standard critical question raised against any proposer of an aristocracy: How do you ensure that the members of the aristocratic class are in fact, and continue to be, the best people? They assumed that a properly organized educational system could both instill virtue in those amenable to it and weed out those whom the system failed to make virtuous. This is not to say that either man was under the illusion that such a system could be made infallible.

I will conclude by touching on a point about which Aristotle says nothing at all. His silence on this issue surprises us, since it represents one of the central concerns of contemporary political thought. This is the question of the boundary between the public and the private. Which of our affairs are none of the government's business? In which of them can it legitimately intervene? Our debates about the purposes of government are primarily arguments about the correct answer to this question. A sign of the importance of the issue is that it is often used to define one of the major dividing lines between contemporary political camps, such as between liberals and conservatives, or Republicans and Democrats.

Aristotle does not address the question of the public and the private spheres. But I don't think he was incapable of making the distinction, or that he would have thought it unimportant. I expect he would readily agree that many matters are best left in the hands of the individual, or the family, or nongovernmental institutions. But he did not try to build such limits on governmental authority into his formula for the purpose of government, except in a very indirect way.

As we have seen, Aristotle's way of determining the purposes of government was to ask about the final cause of the political association in the larger sense. The end of the association determines the end of the apparatus that governs it, since the apparatus exists in order to promote the ends of the association. In his view, the end of political association and hence of government is to foster the happiness of the people. That seems to imply that any measure, any intervention in individual lives that promotes the happiness of the people is to that extent justified, though there may be other considerations arguing against it. However, there is nothing in Aristotle corresponding to the modern conception of inalienable rights. And in the absence of that or something similar, it is hard to see what kind of consideration could outweigh the happiness of the people. Probably the only way to defend maintaining a sphere of privacy against government intervention would be to argue that such intervention would be self-defeating. That is, one would have to argue that public intervention within certain areas, though perhaps contributing in some ways to the good of the society, would in fact work against its happiness in other, more fundamental ways, so that a state which intervened in these areas would be frustrating its own reason for being.

How much of a limit can be imposed on government action by such an argument depends in part on empirical information about the likely consequences of particular actions and policies in particular situations. But it also depends in part on your conception of happiness.

The most important component in happiness, as Aristotle conceived of it, was the development of the ethical and intellectual virtues. Society makes a critical contribution to this development by providing its members with moral and mental training. The government can facilitate and regulate this process in various ways, all of which are subsumed under the heading of education. Education is not only a central concern of the best, aristocratic form of government. It is, or ought to be, Aristotle says, a prime concern of any government. The most important means of preserving a state is to ensure that its citizens receive an education appropriate to its form of government, an education, in other words, that turns them into good citizens (though the good citizen under one form of government will differ in character from the good citizen under another).

To give government a legitimate interest in the development of the character of the citizens is to allow it greater scope than most United States citizens are comfortable with. If government, or society, has an interest in the character of its citizens, it would seem to be justified in regulating anything that affects that character, again subject to the limitation that its actions not be self-defeating. But there is hardly any feature of life that does not arguably have an effect on character. Hence, government control of practically every dimension of life is in principle justifiable.

Such a conclusion will not disturb you if you believe that a government which genuinely promotes the common interest will never have cause to intrude on individual concerns in an obnoxious way, that the common interest will never conflict with respect for what is your business and no one else's, or that the provision that government actions must not be self-defeating provides all the protection against government interference that anyone could want. If that belief strikes you as too optimistic, then you will need a rationale for constraints on government action that Aristotle's political science does not provide.

If we find grounds for criticizing Aristotle on that score, we should also recognize that there is much to be said for the view that society ought to take an interest in the moral education of its members. Modern psychology and sociology have made us aware that we are to a large extent creatures of our social environment. Society does form our character, whether we like it or not, and the only questions are whether this formation will take place haphazardly or under deliberate control; and if under deliberate control, then by what instrumentalities and with what ends in view. Further, while social influence was once regarded as the antithesis of individual autonomy, society being viewed primarily as a threat to the individual's freedom, there has been a change of mood in some circles in recent years. While recognizing the undeniable truth that society can be the enemy of individual liberty, many people have come to believe that it doesn't have to be, that a well-ordered society will in fact be the kind of community in which individuals flourish, and that, being the social creatures we are, it is only in a well-ordered community that we can become fully human. We thus seem to be coming to a deeper appreciation of Aristotle's insight that the human being is by nature a political animal.

Bibliographic Essay

This essay has two purposes: to document the sources of my ideas, and to offer some suggestions for further reading. The former is especially important, since I made no use of footnotes in the text, in hopes of making it easier to read. The two tasks are not unrelated, since nearly everything in the text is taken from Aristotle's own works, and the most important further reading you could do would be in the works of Aristotle. If you've read this book before tackling any of Aristotle's own treatises, that is almost certainly what you should do next.

The surviving works of Aristotle are very concise. It is now generally supposed that they were not intended for publication, but were really just notes Aristotle jotted down to lecture from. That would explain why he so often fails to elaborate on points that perplex us, or to give an example where we need one. It might also account for the fact that he so seldom helps us to see the organization of the works; at times the various chapters or paragraphs seem quite disconnected, and the kinds of transitional remarks and summaries that we have come to expect in expository writing are pretty rare in Aristotle. Moreover, Aristotle often seems to take it for granted, in writing one work, that we have read some of his other works. Occasionally he makes explicit reference to other works, but more often he leaves it to the reader to make the connection. Hopefully, he added a lot when he actually presented these lectures. And maybe in his school, the Lyceum, there was a regular sequence of courses. Unfortunately, that doesn't mean that the problem can be solved by reading the works in the proper order. Someone has said that the best way to understand Aristotle would be to begin your study of him by reading his works for the second time. Since that option isn't available, we must adopt some other course.

As a rule, I dislike the idea of reading bits and pieces of various works rather than attempting a single work in its entirety. But for a first reading of Aristotle, I think that's exactly what you should do. In the first part of what follows, I will indicate the passages in which Aristotle deals specifically with the topics summarized in this book. (The second part deals with secondary sources.) In some cases these citations are to whole chapters; in others, the reference is just to a few lines which contain a particularly clear statement of some doctrine or argument. If you are quite new to Aristotle, I recommend reading only the passages I cite, perhaps returning to the relevant portions of this book for assistance as necessary. In fact, some of these references are just substitutes for footnotes; you can usually recognize these from the context. You could skip those and read only the longer passages. Afterwards, you might want to get a good anthology of selections from Aristotle and read up on what interests you, or you might want to try your hand at an entire treatise. Probably the three easiest to read are the *Poetics*, the *Politics*, and the *Nicomachean Ethics*. I suspect it would be best to delve into additional secondary sources only after some sustained reading of Aristotle, unless you find even the less difficult texts so hard that you want more assistance than this book has provided.

Even if you have some prior exposure to Aristotle's works, I think this plan of action would be a good one. Of course, if you have read a great deal of Aristotle already, then you probably don't need any advice about what to read.

Before I send you off to read Aristotle, I should say a few words about translations. After the description I just gave of Aristotle's works, you can imagine the sort of problems they pose for translators. A literal translation makes for very difficult reading. A translator who makes the text more understandable by filling in the gaps left in the original also interposes more of his or her own interpretation between you and Aristotle's own words. Even the most literal translation involves some interpretation, but the further you get from the literal, the more interpretation there is. The trick is to find the best compromise between strict fidelity to the original, on one hand, and intelligibility, on the other.

If accuracy means literalness, then the most accurate translations of Aristotle are those of Hippocrates G. Apostle and Lloyd P. Gerson, published by the Peripatetic Press of Grinnell, Iowa. In

addition to individual treatises, they have compiled a useful anthology under the title *Aristotle: Selected Works* (1982). I consider
these the best translations for advanced students, such as graduate students with a special interest in ancient philosophy. They
come as close as a translation can to giving you the feel of reading
the original Greek. But they are not the best for beginners, because
they are almost as hard to read as the original. They are equipped
with outlines, glossaries, and indexes. The volumes devoted to
individual sciences also include extensive commentary by the editors, which attempts to fill in gaps and offer possible interpretations or explanations of difficult passages. As a rule, I have found
these less than helpful, and in any event they are omitted from the
anthology. Not all of Aristotle's works are available in this version.

What was for a long time the standard English text was the so-
called "Oxford translation," *The Works of Aristotle*, edited by W. D.
Ross, in twelve volumes (Oxford: Clarendon Press, 1908–1952).
This set, too, included outlines and indexes. Commentary was
confined to footnotes, and these are more copious in some volumes than in others. Different treatises were the work of different
translators, and little effort was made to secure uniformity of terminology. This translation was excerpted in *The Basic Works of
Aristotle*, edited by Richard McKeon (New York: Random House,
1941), who issued an even more condensed version in The Modern
Library under the title *Introduction to Aristotle* (New York: Random House, 1947).

All of these were largely superseded in 1984 when Princeton
University Press published *The Complete Works of Aristotle: The
Revised Oxford Translation*, under the editorship of Jonathan
Barnes. This edition replaced some of the original translations, but
for the most part it consists of slightly revised versions of the texts
edited by Ross. One aim of the revision was to nudge the translations toward greater uniformity, but as Barnes admits, this could
be done only to a limited extent without producing entirely new
translations. As a partial remedy, he includes a brief glossary indicating the range of English words used to translate individual
Greek terms. He also tried to render the translations more literal in
places where the original translators indulged in paraphrase. This
edition omits all the scholarly notes of the first edition, which is
one of the reasons it takes up only two volumes. It also inexplica-

bly eliminates the outlines of the treatises, which didn't take up much space and were quite helpful. Where the original included an index in each of the twelve volumes, the revised edition contains only a single index for the entire two-volume set, with a corresponding reduction in the thoroughness of the indexing. Both the original and the revised editions are easier to read than the Apostle translations.

J. L. Ackrill has edited an anthology called *A New Aristotle Reader* (Princeton, N.J.: Princeton University Press, 1987) which draws in part on the translations in the revised Oxford edition and in part on a series of texts published by Oxford as the Clarendon Aristotle Series. It is thus in effect the successor to the McKeon volumes cited above. This is a good text for beginners. A particularly useful feature is a topical bibliography, which cites both relevant passages in Aristotle and secondary sources. The list of references under each topic is blessedly short, which better suits the initial exploration of a topic than the more customary unclassified and overwhelmingly long bibliographies.

As of this writing, Hackett Publishing Company was projecting publication in the fall of 1995 of a book of selections from Aristotle edited by Gail Fine and Terence Irwin. If Irwin's earlier translation of the *Nicomachean Ethics* is a reliable indicator of the quality of the forthcoming anthology, it will be by far the most readable of such works. It is certainly much more accessible than the Oxford translation in either of its incarnations, and in the process manages to be no less faithful a translation. The advertisement promises both a glossary and an index, and the published table of contents reveals a judicious selection of texts. If it turns out as well as I expect, this would be the anthology of choice for the beginning student of Aristotle.

When you are ready to plunge more deeply into Aristotle's texts, a good set of translations is the Clarendon Aristotle series. These are accompanied by extensive commentary and full bibliographies.

No translation is perfect. If you are willing to take even one course in Greek, you will find yourself in a position to correct some of the more significant defects of translations. If you do no more than learn the Greek alphabet, you will be able to determine when Aristotle (but not his translator) uses the same word in different places and when Aristotle uses different words that the translator has rendered by a single English term. If you are prepared to go that far, you should know about the Loeb Classical Library editions of Aristotle's works, published by Harvard University Press. These editions print the Greek text and an English translation on facing pages. The translations are of uneven quality; but they make it easier for the novice in Greek to find the Greek words in which a crucial point is expressed.

SOURCES

This part of the essay is meant to document, with some specificity, the sources of my account of Aristotle's philosophy. Most of my references are to Aristotle's own works. All but the shortest of Aristotle's treatises are divided into "books" (corresponding to parchment rolls in the very earliest editions), which are further subdivided into chapters. Reference by book and chapter isn't specific enough for many purposes, and it also suffers from the disadvantage that different editors put the books in different orders and divide them into chapters in different ways. Scholars have therefore created a uniform system of citation based on the first modern edition of the Greek text of Aristotle's works, *Aristotelis Opera*, edited by Immanuel Bekker and published in Berlin by G. Reimer between 1831 and 1870. Each page in this edition has two columns, and the lines in each column are numbered. All the better translations print Bekker's page numbers, column indicators (a or b), and line numbers in their margins. The standard method for citing Aristotle is to give the title of the work in question, followed by the book number in Roman numerals, the chapter number in Arabic numerals, and then page, column, and line of the location in Bekker. Thus, *"Posterior Analytics I, 2, 71b10–72b4"* directs you to the first book, second chapter of that work, and specifically to the text running from page 71, column b, line 10, to page 72, column b, line 4, of the Bekker edition. The book and chapter are often handy to have, even though they aren't entirely reliable. The Bekker number, on the other hand, can be counted on to take you to exactly the same passage, no matter what edition or translation of Aristotle you are using. There is one qualification to that statement, however. The lines in translations never coincide exactly with lines in the Greek text, so the line numbers must be taken as approximate.

The citations in this essay are based on the book and chapter divisions found in Apostle's translations. Because the Bekker numbers get so cumbersome, I often cite only book and chapter when the passage of interest occupies all or most of a chapter. Where this principle would lead me to cite only book and chapter, but Apostle's chapter numbering differs from that of other editors (especially that of the revised Oxford translation), I have added in parentheses the Bekker number indicating the beginning of the chapter I cite. For the most part, the order of my citations follows the order in which the ideas are presented in the text.

Wisdom and Science

Scientific knowledge, intuition, and wisdom are among the intellectual virtues dicussed in book VI of the *Nicomachean Ethics*. Science is dealt with in chapter 3, intuition in chapter 6, and wisdom in chapter 7. The definition of wisdom on which my exposition is based is found in chapter 7, at 1141a19–20. A lengthier discussion of wisdom occurs in the first two chapters of the *Metaphysics*. Metaphysics is the discipline which investigates the "most valuable things," so it more than any other science qualifies as the quest for wisdom. The word "metaphysics" was actually coined by an ancient editor of Aristotle's works. Aristotle himself called the kind of knowledge sought in that discipline either "wisdom," or "first philosophy" (in the sense of the most fundamental philosophic discipline), or "theology" (since it includes discussion of the unmoved movers). The description of scientific knowledge in the *Nicomachean Ethics* is pretty sketchy. For more detail, including an account of demonstration, see the *Posterior Analytics*, particularly I, 2, 71b10–72b4.

The distinctions between genus and species and between first and second substances will be found in *Categories* 5, 2a12–19. As I indicated in the text, there is some disagreement about what Aristotle finally considered the prime examples of substances. If you want to explore this topic further, you might start with Michael Loux, *Primary* Ousia: *An Essay on Aristotle's* Metaphysics *VII–IX* (Ithaca, N.Y.: Cornell University Press, 1991). This has the advantage that Loux meant it to be intelligible to readers who aren't specialists in Greek philosophy. The introduction gives a particularly clear account of the point at issue, and there is a bibliography to direct you to other works on the topic.

The explanation I give as to why individuals cannot be the subjects of a science is taken from *Metaphysics* VII, 15, 1039b27–1040a2. A different line of reasoning occurs at *Posterior Analytics* I, 31, 87b29–40.

THE FOUR CAUSES

The causes are inventoried in several places, and since they are not always described in the same way, the student who is really serious about Aristotle may find it worthwhile to compare the different formulations. The relevant passages are *Physics* II, 3, 194b17–195a4; *Physics* II, 7, 198a14–69; *Metaphysics* I, 3, 983a24–33; *Generation of Animals* I, 1, 715a5–12; *Posterior Analytics* II, 11, 94a20–24. What strikes me as the clearest general statement of what Aristotle means by a final cause is in *Parts of Animals* I, 1, 641b24–26. In some passages, Aristotle distinguishes two senses of "final cause," but the proper interpretation of this distinction is not clear, and you will find it rendered differently in different translations. See *On the Soul* II, 4, 415b3–4 (repeated at 415b21–22) and *Metaphysics* XII, 7, 1072b2–4. The principle that cause and effect are simultaneous or, more accurately, that the activity of the agent and that of the thing acted on are simultaneous, is stated at *On the Soul* III, 2, 425b27.

THE VOCABULARY OF SCIENCE

Physics II, 1, 192b9–193a1 gives the definition of "nature," as well as explicating the meanings of common phrases containing that term ("by nature," "according to nature"). The relationship between nature and final cause is dealt with in *Physics* II, 8, with a particularly clear explication of "what exists by nature" at 199b16–17. Various senses of the Greek word for "nature" are inventoried in the "philosophical lexicon" of book V of the *Metaphysics*. The primary sense of the term, and hence the one most important for Aristotle, is stated at 1015a14–19.

The relationship between prime matter and the elements is laid out in *On Generation and Destruction* II, 1, 329a6–b6. A discussion of the controversy surrounding that issue can be found in the appendix to C.J.F. Williams's translation of that work, published under its Latin title, *De Generatione et Corruptione* (Oxford: Clarendon Press, 1982). For a more extensive and more recent treatment, see Mary Louise Gill, *Aristotle on Substance: The Paradox of Unity* (Princeton, N.J.: Princeton University Press, 1989), with its substantial bibliography.

The primary text for my interpretation of "essence" and "essential attribute" is *Posterior Analytics* I, 4, 73a35–b24. "Definition" and "property" (along with "genus" and "accident") are discussed in the *Topics*, with the distinctions drawn most clearly perhaps in I, 5. That a definition consists of genus and difference is rather assumed than explicitly stated through most of that treatise; he finally says this in so many words at VI, 4, 141b26–7. The characterization of a definition as "the formula of the essence" is back at I, 5, 101b39, and also in *Posterior Analytics* II, 10, 93b30.

The Form of Scientific Explanation

Aristotle's categories, with his own examples of terms that fall under each category, are listed in the treatise of the same name, in chapter 4. Syllogisms are discussed extensively in the *Prior Analytics,* and demonstration in the *Posterior Analytics.* Book I, chapter 2 of the *Posterior Analytics* lays out the connection between demonstration and scientific knowledge, and goes into some detail about the criteria which the premises of an argument must satisfy if the argument is to count as a demonstration. These are the criteria that I summed up under the headings of "necessity" and "self-evidence." There, too, you will find the assertion that the principles of a science must be indemonstrable. That the middle term is the primary object of scientific investigation is made plain in *Posterior Analytics* II, 2.

Aristotle's views about how we come to know the principles of the sciences must be pieced together from several sources. One difficulty is that Aristotle does not clearly distinguish the process of forming a general concept from that of discovering a general principle. Perhaps this is because he often thinks of scientific principles as nothing other than definitions. (He says as much at

Posterior Analytics II, 3, 90b24–25 and *On the Soul* I, 1, 402b26. Compare also the statement at *Nicomachean Ethics* VI, 9, 1142a26, that intuition is of definitions.) A definition can be thought of as a proposition which spells out the content of a general concept, so if all scientific principles are definitions, then the distinction between concepts and propositions may not be important for understanding how we arrive at these things. *Posterior Analytics* I, 2, 72a7–22, on the other hand, seems to distinguish definitions from other sorts of first principles, and Aristotle's examples of principles in chapters 10 and 11 of that book clearly include things other than definitions (among them, the example I gave in my text).

Nicomachean Ethics VI, 3 says that it is by induction that we arrive at universals and acquire principles. "Universal" can refer either to a general term or concept, or to a general proposition; "principle," likewise, in Aristotelian usage, can denote a concept or a proposition (in addition to some other things). *Metaphysics* I, 1 traces an evolution from sensation to memory to experience to science or art, and identifies the latter with knowledge of universal propositions (Aristotle's example is the principle that such-and-such a medicine or therapy benefits anyone who suffers from such-and-such a disease). The same progression is related in *Posterior Analytics* II, 19, 99b31–100b7, but is there depicted as resulting in such concepts as "human being" and "such-and-such an animal." It explicitly refers to this process as "induction." *Prior Analytics* II, 23, 68b15–25, illustrates what Aristotle means by "induction," and in this case it leads to a generalization. *Topics* I, 2 makes the discovery of scientific principles the business of dialectic, and chapter 12 of the same book says that dialectic makes use of both induction and syllogisms, as if these were two quite distinct kinds of reasoning; but the passage just cited from the *Prior Analytics* seems to describe an inductive syllogism. The passage from the *Posterior Analytics* cited previously is followed by one (100b7–18) which identifies "intuition" as the faculty by which scientific principles are known. (The same claim is made, at a slightly further remove from discussion of induction, in *Nicomachean Ethics* VI, 6.) In the context, we must take this to mean that it is either the faculty of carrying out an induction or the faculty by which the result of an induction is held in the mind. Though Aristotle does not say which, I think the latter is more likely. That fits better with my interpretation of intuition as a kind of direct awareness of the principles which is in some sense self-certifying—the kind of thing that led me to characterize the principles as "self-evident." But it also agrees better with the fact that Aristotle also applies the term "intuition" to sensation. All that sensation and intellectual grasp of a principle would seem to have in common is the immediacy of these two forms of awareness.

My interpretation of intuition as involving an awareness of the explanatory power of a principle is based in part on *On the Soul* I, 1, 402b18–403a3, and in part on Aristotle's practice in his scientific treatises. A particularly accessible example of this is *Nicomachean Ethics* I, 8–9, 1098b10–1099b8, where Aristotle defends his definition of happiness on the grounds that it accounts for the "data" about happiness reflected in widely held opinions.

What Wisdom Knows

Actuality and potentiality are discussed at great length and with little clarity in books VIII and IX of the *Metaphysics*. The key text for my exposition is chapter 6 of book IX, especially the series of examples Aristotle gives at 1048a37–b7. The distinction I make between active and passive potencies is based on book IX, chapter 1, 1046a20–29. Aristotle's definition of change is stated at *Physics* III, 1, 201a11–12. The principle that a form can be imposed only on an appropriate matter can be found at several places in Aristotle's works. See, for example, *Physics* II, 2, 194b9; *On the Soul* II, 2, 414a26–28; and *Metaphysics* IX, 7, 1048b33–1049a18.

The main source for Aristotle's views about the soul is naturally the treatise *On the Soul*. His definition of the soul and analysis of its parts, together with a first broaching of the question of immortality, are found in book II, chapters 1 and 2. Immortality is taken up again in book III, chapters 4 and 5. That's where you'll find the arguments for the separability of the passive intellect from the body, and for the immortality of the agent intellect. The *Nicomachean Ethics* has its own way of characterizing the parts of the soul for ethical purposes. That's in chapter 13 of book I.

The unmoved movers are dealt with in both the *Physics* and the *Metaphysics*, and naturally there is room for disagreement over whether the two treatments are compatible. I recommend sampling the *Physics* VIII, 1, 250b10–251b10, and 6, 258b10–259a13; then from book XII of the *Metaphysics*, read chapter 1, 1069a31–b2, as a kind of preface, and afterwards work through all of chapters 6–9.

ETHICS

On first reading, Aristotle's treatises on ethics and politics seem disjointed. A coherent pattern begins to emerge only as you begin to recognize what Aristotle is taking for granted, the background assumptions which define his viewpoint on these matters. Much of my chapters on these topics is therefore devoted to articulating these assumptions as I understand them. You would search in vain for explicit statements of these in his own works.

The first two books of the *Nicomachean Ethics* lay out the basic principles of this discipline. Book I revolves around the definition of happiness; Aristotle's own definition is given in chapter 6, at 1098a16–17. If you're just after the essentials, I think you could skip chapters 4 (1096a12), 7 (1098a21), 11 (1100a10), and 12 (1101b10). The discussion of virtue begins with the last chapter (13), which contains the distinction between ethical and intellectual virtues, and continues through book II. The definition of virtue occurs in chapter 6 of that book (1106b36–1107a2). An indication of the kinds of circumstances that determine where the mean lies can be found in the same chapter at 1107a14–18, and also in chapter 9, at 1108a27–28. Chapter 7 gives a brief catalog of the ethical virtues and their corresponding vices. More elaborate treatments of these begin at chapter 9 (1115a5) of book III and extend through books IV and V, with the entirety of book V being devoted to justice. Book VI surveys the intellectual virtues. Book X, chapters 6 through 9, defends the claim that the intellectual life is the happiest. My outline pays little attention to the topic of friendship, but Aristotle devotes two books (VIII and IX) of the *Nicomachean Ethics* to it. Apart from its intrinsic interest, friendship has political implications, since, as I noted in the text, the Greek notion is broader than ours and includes the kind of solidarity one might feel for one's fellow-citizens. On this point, see especially chapters 11 through 13 of book VIII (1159b25–1161b10).

POLITICS

My estimates of the size and population of the Greek states are taken from *The World of Athens: An Introduction to Classical Athenian Culture*, produced by the Joint Association of Classical Teachers (Cambridge: Cambridge University Press, 1984). This is a fine introduction to all aspects of ancient Greek culture. It presumes no prior knowledge, covers a wide range of topics, and picks out the details that are interesting, rather than overwhelming you with "all you need to know." That Athens is always at the center of focus will not be a disadvantage for most readers.

The reader of the *Politics* should start at the beginning, with the first two chapters of book I. Aristotle there identifies the genus of the state and its end, and explains why human beings are political animals. In book III, chapter 6, Aristotle explains what a "form of government" is and makes the basic distinction between good and deviant forms. Chapter 7 enumerates the six basic forms. There is also a brief and clear discussion of the six forms and the difference between good and bad forms in the *Nicomachean Ethics*, VIII, 12. In III, 8 of the *Politics*, Aristotle explains why forms of government should be classifed by what segment of society is in control, rather than by what proportion of the populace exercises power. Chapters 9–13 of book III discuss the pros and cons of various forms in a general way. The different senses of the expression "best form of government" are distinguished in book IV, chapter 1.

That aristocracy is the best form of government is seldom stated in so many words. I think the earliest place in which it is clearly implied is III, 13, 1248a2–4. A more explicit statement occurs at III, 18, 1288a33–38, and again at IV, 2, 1289a31–34. Here and elsewhere Aristotle lumps aristocracy and monarchy together as "the" best form. He seems almost to regard monarchy as a variant of aristocracy, for both consist in rule by the most virtuous, and he thinks monarchy appropriate only when some one person is far more virtuous than anyone else in the state, for it would not be just for one person to hold exclusive authority over his or her equals in virtue. (See III, 17, 1288a9–19; and III, 16, 1287a17–19.) From the way he talks about this, I get the impression Aristotle thought that such a state of affairs was rare. (See, for example, III, 13, 1284a4–17, though Aristotle may here be reporting on a common opinion rather than expressing his own.)

It is in chapter 11 of book IV that Aristotle defends *politeia* as the best form of government for most states. His discussion of slavery will be found back in the first book, chapters 4–7. The disqualification of artisans and laborers from participation in government is discussed in book III, chapter 5, 1278a3–21. Farmers are added to the list in VIII, 9, 1328b34–1329a2. Aristotle's description of the ideal state occupies books VII and VIII, with book VIII containing the unfinished treatment of the system of education in that state.

SUGGESTIONS FOR FURTHER READING

There are many books that could be classified as introductions to Aristotle's thought, though what the word "introduction" implies depends on the author's assessment of the audience he or she is aiming at. Hardly anyone other than a teacher of Aristotle would want to read all of them, but since they vary in both breadth and complexity and also in their angle of approach, I'll discuss several of them here to help you decide which one or two are best for you.

Some of these are more accessible and more superficial than *Aristotle in Outline*, so you should consult those only if you found something in this text particularly difficult. In this category are Mortimer Adler, *Aristotle for Everybody* (New York: Macmillan, 1978) and Jonathan Barnes, *Aristotle* (New York: Oxford University Press, 1982). Adler's book is misleading on some points, particularly on the final cause and on Aristotle's political philosophy, but it is certainly easy to read. In fact, he originally considered calling it *Aristotle for Children*. I would avoid Barnes's book. I find many of his explanations inadequate or misleading, and he seems fonder of pointing out where Aristotle is wrong than of inquiring into the possible rationale for his supposedly erroneous doctrines.

The works you should really be interested in are those that go into greater depth than this one. The clearest of these, and the one nearest to this one in spirit, is Jonathan Lear, *Aristotle: The Desire to Understand* (New York: Cambridge University Press, 1988). I think it is as readable as *Aristotle in Outline*; in fact, since he devotes more time to each topic, he is probably even clearer in some places than I am. He goes into more detail than I do and tells you more about Aristotle's relationships to other philosophers.

At a slightly greater level of difficulty are D. J. Allan, *The Phi-*

losophy of Aristotle, 2d ed. (New York: Oxford University Press, 1970) and J. L. Ackrill, *Aristotle the Philosopher* (New York: Oxford University Press, 1981). Allan gives a straightforward account of Aristotle's doctrines and arguments. Ackrill engages Aristotle in a more critical way, deliberately viewing Aristotle through the eyes of a twentieth-century philosopher and often trying to imagine how Aristotle would respond to the objections such a philosopher would raise. He does this, however, without ceasing to read Aristotle sympathetically (differing in this from Barnes), and the result is quite satisfactory. Given this approach, the book is more likely to appeal to a reader with some philosophic training, but I wouldn't say it demands that.

Marjorie Grene, *A Portrait of Aristotle* (Chicago: University of Chicago Press, 1963) takes Aristotle's biological investigations as the key to his philosophic methods. This is accordingly a good introduction for anyone with an interest in biology or natural history, and it offers a sound counterargument to those who accuse Aristotle of being insufficiently empirical.

John Herman Randall, *Aristotle* (New York: Columbia University Press, 1960) approaches the philosopher from the perspective of American Pragmatism. He is quite enthusiastic (but not gushy) about Aristotle, and he is not ashamed to admit to perplexity on some points. This combination of qualities makes the book a pleasure to read. I found some of his discussions quite valuable, particularly the chapter on "First Philosophy."

W. D. Ross, *Aristotle*, 5th ed. (New York: Methuen, 1953) presents a point-by-point summary of the major treatises. There is almost no criticism, and he makes no concessions to the beginning reader, but it is packed with information.

For the reader with some philosophic training, particularly in contemporary philosophy, Abraham Edel, *Aristotle and His Philosophy* (Chapel Hill, N.C.: University of North Carolina Press, 1982) offers a comprehensive survey which emphasizes the interconnectedness of Aristotle's thought on different topics. Edel is particularly good at relating Aristotle's views to those of other thinkers. He is also keenly aware, and makes his reader aware, of the hazards of interpreting an historical text, and you come away from his book with greater confidence in your ability to assess the plausibility of such interpretations.

During the middle decades of this century, Aristotle studies

were profoundly influenced by Werner Jaeger's work attempting
to trace the evolution of Aristotle's thought. His theses were always controversial and have largely fallen out of favor now, but
you may come across traces of them or references to them even in
the contemporary literature. If you want to check these out at the
source, see his *Aristotle: Fundamentals of the History of His Development*, tr. Richard Robinson (Oxford: Clarendon Press, 1934). If
you're just curious and want a quick summary, the article
"Aristotle" in the *Encyclopedia of Philosophy*, ed. Paul Edwards
(New York: Macmillan, 1967) covers it in one page.

When you're ready to go beyond even the more sophisticated
introductions and surveys, the best approach might be to look into
some journal articles on the aspects of Aristotle's thought that interest you most. The notes and bibliographies of the introductory
works I have cited will give you some guidance here. Perhaps the
best starting point would be *Articles on Aristotle*, ed. Jonathan
Barnes, Malcolm Schofield, and Richard Sorabji, 4 vols. (London:
Duckworth, 1975–79). These volumes assemble a great many of
the more illuminating articles on a variety of topics. They are organized by subject. For articles published since then, the "topic references" in Ackrill's *New Aristotle Reader* (Princeton, N.J.: Princeton
University Press, 1987) are quite handy, because the number of
references is quite limited. They direct you to both journal articles
and individual chapters in books. For even more recent citations,
consult the *Philosopher's Index*.

Most of the introductory works offer a sketch of Aristotle's life.
I think Edel and Ross are particularly good.

Index